HYPNOTIC
SELLING
SECRETS

HYPNOTIC SELLING SECRETS

TRIGGER YOUR BUYER'S SUBCONSCIOUS

DR. JOE VITALE

Published 2022 by Gildan Media LLC
aka G&D Media
www.GandDmedia.com

Front cover design by David Rheinhardt of Pyrographx

Interior design by Meghan Day Healey of Story Horse, LLC

Library of Congress Cataloging-in-Publication Data is available upon
request

ISBN: 978-1-7225-0574-5

10   9   8   7   6   5   4   3   2   1

To Robert Collier

Contents

1

What Is Hypnotic Writing?

I got a FedEx package recently, and I want to read the letter that came with it. First of all, it came by FedEx, so that was pretty attention-getting in itself. There was a $20 bill attached to it, which was pretty attention-getting too.

It began, "Dear Joe Vitale: I have an offer that I would like to share with only you that will make you a stack of those $20 bills in one to two weeks. Before I go on, let me explain why I'm sending this to you. "My name is _____. I am in a jam and need to make $10,000 before the end of the month.

"There are three reasons why I need this. One, to keep a promise to a close friend. I told a close friend that I would have a motorcycle before he gets back from his deployment in the desert." He goes on to explain that. "Two, I made some bad decisions with money a while back and I'm currently very tight with money"—in other words, broke. "Three, I'm on vacation from the thirteenth of this month till the twenty-ninth and I would like to be able to do something over that time period. I would at least like to be able to visit my grandparents in Fort Worth and have enough money to enjoy it." He tells me where he lives. He goes on to say that he wants to create a joint venture with me.

On the second page, he describes himself as a marketing specialist. He says he wants me to send out a mailing to my list looking for people who want his services. He says, "I will charge a retainer fee up front anywhere from $5,000 to $25,000, depending on how much of a profit I think I could make for their business: anywhere from 5 to 50 percent of the profits generated. The retainer will be paid off on the back-end profits." Then he goes on to say, "I will give you 50 percent of all the profits."

One of his postscripts says, "If you are wondering why there is a $20 bill attached to the top of this letter, it is because I hope to be sending you a large stack of them in the next several weeks."

My question to you is, is this a hypnotic letter?

To me, this is not a hypnotic letter. In fact, it's a terrible letter. I sent his $20 back because he says he's broke. The only reason I didn't burn this is that I needed his address on the back of the second letter so I could send the money back.

Why isn't it a hypnotic letter? He got my attention, which is one of the key ingredients for writing good copy. He FedExed it to me—$20, very eye-catching. It begins well: "I have an offer that I would like to share with only you that will make you a stack of those $20 bills in one to two weeks." That's good. He's speaking to me, but from there, it's all about him.

The first statement said he wants to buy a motorcycle. I don't care if he needs a motorcycle. He wants to buy it because he made a promise to a friend. I don't care that he made a promise to a friend. The second one is, he's made bad decisions about money. He's broke. I don't care about that. I might care if he told me it in different terms, but a lot of people are broke. He's telling me he's broke, and he wants to do something that's off the wall. Third is, he's on vacation. I don't care if he's on vacation. He wants to make use of his vacation time and make some money. Then he's asking me to do a mailing to my list and he's claiming he's a marketing specialist.

Where's the proof that he's a marketing specialist? This is doubtful. I'm thinking this guy doesn't know what he's talking about. Then he wants to charge people on my list $5,000 to $25,000 to do marketing, which is what *I* do. Why would I send my people to him and let him get half of the money, which all should go to me? None of this makes sense.

Of course, his postscript is pretty good. But it's powerless at that point, because he lost me with this self-serving stuff.

Now there are terrible letters out there all over the place. I want to tell you how to write your sales letters, your web copy, and anything else that you're writing in a riveting way. This is where hypnotic copywriting comes in.

In this book, I'm going to reveal, for the first time ever, my own system for writing hypnotic copy. I've written a lot of books, but I've never revealed how I personally sit down and write.

I don't want you to become a Joe Vitale clone and start writing the way Joe writes. But I want you to take on some of these elements, and I want you to learn this formula that I use, and then adapt it for yourself. When I was a teenager, I met Rod Serling, of *The Twilight Zone*. That was a turning point in my life, and it was disappointing. I thought Rod Serling was going to be a god, a superhuman. He wrote incredible material for *The Twilight Zone* and *Night Gallery*; he was a brilliant scriptwriter, a hypnotic storyteller. But he was a little runt of a guy, chain-smoking, very human.

I asked him, "What would you write about in your auto-biography?" and he said, "I don't think I've done anything."

He dismissed his life, his career, and everything that he had done, so he decided he wasn't going to write his autobiography. Of course, when he died, somebody wrote a biography of him, so his life was worth writing about, but he didn't think so. I thought, if he can do this and succeed at being a writer, then I can too, and that was a turning point for me.

When I was a teenager back in Ohio, I saw an ad for a famous writers' school. I filled out the form and sent it in, and one of their representatives came to my house. He said, "Wouldn't it be great to be able to write like Rod Serling?"

"Yeah," I said, "that would be great—to write like Rod Serling."

"No, no," he said. "You don't want to write like Rod Serling. You want to write like Joe Vitale."

That's what I want you to do: gather different methods and fine-tune what you're already doing. Try on my own method of writing copy and then make it your own.

I love to set an intention for just about everything that I do, and I would invite you to set an intention for what you want to achieve with this book. What do you want to receive? What do you want to experience? What do you want to learn? Where do you want to be mentally?

Where do you want to be physically? I'm going to invite you to write this down now.

1. What do you want to achieve with this book?

_____

_____

_____

2. What would be better than what you're thinking right now? If you start by thinking, "I want to be able to write website copy that gets a 25 percent response," what would be better than that? An obvious answer might be something that gets a 35 percent response. I'm asking you to stretch. I'm asking you to think really big—bigger than you've ever thought before.

_____

_____

_____

Once I read about a woman who has six children, thirty-five grandchildren, seventy-five great grandchildren, and ten great, great grandchildren. She jumped from an airplane to celebrate her ninety-third birthday. That's a woman who thinks big.

In 1925, ad man Bruce Barton wrote a fundraising letter that got a 100 percent response. Is that good? That's miraculous.

There is a hospital in India, the Aravind Eye Hospital. It started with eleven beds; it is now the largest eye care facility in the world. They see over 1.4 million patients and perform over 200,000 sight-restoring surgeries each year. Two-thirds of their patients don't have to pay a penny. Those who do pay, pay around $75. That was thinking big. The man who started it had what was probably considered an impossible dream. But now it is a reality: the largest eye care center in the world.

What's your intention for this book? Maybe it's to learn how to write sales letters, but maybe you can enlarge that and make it much more powerful, even earthshaking.

I am encouraging you to write down your mission, your goal. What is your intention? What do you intend to learn from this book?

I have found that if you want to really make a difference, if you want to achieve goals that are impossible or majestic or miraculous, have a goal that doesn't influence you alone: you want to have a goal that influences other people. José Silva, creator of the Silva Mind Control Method, said, "You want to state a goal or an intention that helps at least two other people besides you."

If you follow this advice, one magical thing that happens is that it gets you out of your ego. I have found that as soon as you step out of your ego, you get more power from the universe itself. As soon as you have a goal that influences many other people, you have a lot of support from what might be called the invisible.

From the psychological standpoint, you also escape self-sabotage. If you want to have a goal that influences you alone, it's easy to sabotage your own efforts. Some part of you knows that this is only for you. The guy who wrote the letter I mentioned at the beginning of this chapter sabotaged his own efforts just by the way he wrote it. Something in him was communicating that it was only about him.

In this book, you'll learn how I write copy, and you'll learn my twenty-one-point checklist for reviewing copy. You'll be looking at copy very differently—your own and everybody else's.

From time to time, somebody will say, "I hate selling" or "I hate marketing." If I probe a little bit to ask them why, I tend to find that they have a mindset saying that it needs to be done in a particular way.

I'm known as an Internet marketer; some say I'm one of the pioneers of Internet marketing. I more or less fell into it, because I didn't go in as a marketing person. I went in as a person who shared his excitement for products that he fell in love with. That's basically what I do. This is what I think marketing really is.

It's like seeing a movie that you're really excited about it, and you go and tell your friends. You're marketing that movie, you're selling them on that movie, but it never occurs to you.

Forget all about copywriting. Forget all about marketing. Come from sharing your excitement for your mission. Share what you're excited about. Why are you excited about it? Who is it for? Share your enthusiasm with that target audience; that's when the sales take place. Other people will say, "That was smart marketing." In your mind, you'll know: "I was just sharing something I love."

That is one of my secrets to writing the kind of copy I write. I get excited about something. I sit down. I write out my excitement, and I share it. There was a fellow named Mike Mograbi, who had a book called *378 Internet Marketing Predictions*. He wrote to me several times asking me to review it. I kept saying, "I'm busy, not right now." He was very polite but persistent.

I finally looked at his book. It was in two volumes. I was blown away. I was in awe, excited, enthused about it. Within two hours of finishing his book, I wrote to him and asked, "Can I be an affiliate for this?" He wrote immediately back and set it up for me. Fifteen minutes after that, I wrote a quick sales letter telling people how excited I was about this book, and I sent out the letter.

The next day, I was still on a rush from the book. I kept looking at it and thought, "I didn't know about all of this different stuff that's happening, and I'm an Internet person. I live on the Internet; I should know this, but I don't. If I don't know this, my list probably doesn't either."

I sent out another email the next day saying, "Look, I hope you understand how serious I am about this. You may have deleted the letter from yesterday, but these two volumes are so important that I'm sending another letter out right now."

I got sales, but this was not a marketing strategy. It was not something Joe did by premeditation. I did not think, "What is the best way to market this book? What is the best way to write the sales letter?" I thought, "I want to tell my list about this." Then I set up a teleseminar with this guy. Of course I sent out an email about that.

Do you see the key ingredient? I was excited. I wanted to share something I believed in. That's another key to hypnotic writing: sincerity. Too many writers are trying to deceive, manipulate, persuade, and be cute with people instead of sharing their own natural excitement in their own natural voice.

In a way, I've just given you the definition of hypnotic copywriting: sharing your own natural excitement in your own natural voice. The people that are ready for your product or service are the ones that are going to buy. You're not going to be a street corner preacher just trying to gather up anybody. You're going after the people that are going to be interested in your product or service.

This process can be easy. One of my messages is to strip away everything that you learned in school about writing, grammar, punctuation, all of the things that your second- or third-grade teacher told you about writing, because most of that stops our creativity today; it stops us from communicating naturally.

Mark Twain has a famous quote: "If we were all taught to speak the same way we were taught to write, we'd all stutter." Most of us, when we start writing, start editing. We write a few words and cross them out. We'll write a paragraph and think, "That's not really saying what I wanted to say." We judge our writing while we're in the middle of it, when we are not at our clearest or most objective.

Share your enthusiasm. Forget writing. Forget grammar. (There is a place for that. I'll tell you about it later.) Let it be easy.

There's a little booklet called *Afformations*, by Noah St. John. Affirmations, of course, are positive statements that you would say to yourself, like, "I am calm and confident." Afformations, by contrast, are changed into *why* statements. You ask a why question of yourself, which engages your brain to go looking for the answer. An example might be, "Why did I learn how to write sales letters that now gets a 50–60 percent response rate?"

You put the *why?* in there. This gives your brain a direction. The brain is our search and find tool. It's a great radar system, but you have to ask the right question. Ask why. Then your mind starts to look for the answer. You can surprise yourself by what you find.

Here's one secret that a lot of copywriters use, especially if they have trouble writing a sales letter and aren't finding the right way to articulate what they want to say. They'll call somebody on the phone. They'll tell them about the product or the service that they're trying to describe. They will record the conversation. They will look at the transcript, because they will often automatically say some words to express the concept that weren't coming to them when they were writing.

Some people are much more comfortable speaking than writing. If this is true for you, speak, record your speech, transcribe it, and edit it, or even get an editor to do it. This goes back to the theme of *easy*: this can be profoundly easy. It does not have to be hard in any way, shape, or form.

You an also use engaging questions. One of my favorite ways to write a headline is to ask a question that people cannot answer without reading the copy below.

What is hypnotic writing? Part of the answer is that it's writing that you can't put down. You have to finish reading it to satisfy your curiosity. Of course, that could be a work of fiction, which isn't asking you to buy anything. In the case of ad copy, it's writing you can't put down that leads to a sale.

Hypnotic writing involves what's called a *waking trance*. The most familiar form of hypnosis is when the hypnotist puts you under, you close your eyes, and you relax. In a waking trance, you are in a similar state, but your eyes are open. Although this technique is used a great deal in hypnosis, not much has been written about it. The late Dave Elman was a famous hypnotist who mentioned waking trances in his book *Findings in Hypnosis*.

You can go into a waking trance with many forms of writing: novels, articles, sales letters, and short stories, such as *Martin Eden*, a semiautobiographical novel by Jack London.

At the end, Martin Eden commits suicide by drowning himself. He jumps into the ocean. He finds that when you jump into the ocean and drown yourself, your body tries to survive. It tries to come back up. Drowning yourself is not an easy thing to do. In two paragraphs, London describes the thought process and the physical process that Martin Eden went through in order to commit suicide in the ocean. I probably read that thirty years ago, and I still get chills remembering it. He put me in a waking trance. When I was reading that, my eyes were open, I was awake, but nothing else around me mattered. I was with Martin Eden.

I'm often asked whether hypnotic writing is ethical. Sister Mary Elizabeth was a nun at the Vatican, working directly with the pope. Once my wife and I went to Rome.

We went to the Vatican to meet with Sister Mary Elizabeth. We had a wonderful lunch with her. They gave us so much—homemade wine; it was a three-hour meal. They gave us gifts to take home. I kept saying, "What can I do for you?"

Sister Mary Elizabeth said, "We're thanking *you*."

"For what?"

"We've used your hypnotic writing methods to write fundraising letters that have raised money to feed the homeless and starving children in some of the worst places on the planet." I had no idea. She gave us a ride back to our hotel room. On the way, she said, "I didn't believe that hypnotic writing would work, but I tried it, and it absolutely did. We raised money from people that we weren't getting it from before."

The people I've worked with have been ethical. I don't think any of them are trying to do something that's illegal or immoral or unethical. They know they've got a great cause.

They're all doing wonderful things in the world. We're looking for the best way to communicate those wonderful things to the people who want to hear about them. It's absolutely ethical.

A 1956 course called *Dynamic Speed Hypnosis* says that anything you do that makes your listeners react because of mental images you plant in their mind is waking hypnosis.

Here's my working definition: *hypnotic writing is intentionally using words to guide people into a focused mental state where they are inclined to buy your product or service.*

When I was first working up this definition, I was playing with a different word for "inclined." I thought, of saying "a mental state where they are led to buy your product or service" or "made to buy your product or service." But I thought, that's not really what I'm doing. I'm not making anybody do anything. There's no guarantee that they're going to do what I suggest. Instead, I thought, I'm going to lead them to the point where they can make an informed decision. They'll probably be inclined to buy the product or service.

I would be misleading you if I said the process would be automatic. Even though my sales letters get great response, it's almost unheard of to get a 100 percent response. You're not going to persuade everybody. That's just a fact.

The List and the Offer

Some people put too much emphasis on copywriting. They think by having the sales letter, they're going to save they're business. But that is not the case. The sales letter will help and might make a difference, but at least two other elements go into this three-piece puzzle.

The first is your *list* (or your traffic, if you're talking about online sales). If you're writing something and sending it to a list that has no interest in it whatsoever, that hypnotic letter of yours is not going to sell anything. Many people make that mistake and then blame the sales letter.

Well, who did you send it to? There has to be a match. This is the most important thing—more important than either of the other two elements. Who is getting the letter? That's the number one thing.

The second element is your *offer*. What's the deal? You have to make a deal that they can't get somewhere else. Almost certainly you've got competition of one sort or another. How is your offer better than what's already out there?

The copy is important, but it's not the most important thing. Here I'm trying to defuse all the energy we put on the copywriting, because I want it to be easy for you. If you put too much pressure on it, it won't be.

The Hypnotic Agreement

I want to talk about the parallels between hypnosis and writing. In hypnosis, there is something called the *agreement*. This means that when you go to a hypnotist, you've unconsciously told yourself that they could hypnotize you. You didn't sign anything that said that, but there was an unconscious agreement there. Otherwise you wouldn't have gone to that hypnotist.

Similarly, a sales letter won't get automatic attention unless a previous relationship is in place. In other words, if you send out sales letters, you have a built-in relationship with the people receiving it. If you've maintained that relationship, you have the effect of an agreement. That's a start. That means there's a bit of a rapport already there. They're giving you a nod. They'll pay attention to what you're sending them.

The next thing you want to do is get attention. Hypnotists have to get you to focus your attention before they can influence you. They use everything from a little spiral to a flashing light to focusing on a spot on the wall. Similarly, a sales letter has to get your attention before you will read it. Most of the time this is done with the headline.

Here are some other parallels between hypnotism and hypnotic writing:

Rapport. A hypnotist has to lead you into a deeper trance by repetition, by relaxing you, and by keeping you focused. A sales letter has to lead you to want the product by focusing on benefits, using repetition, and keeping your mind on this one target.

Strengthening. A hypnotist has to deepen your trance by asking you to go deeper and relax more fully, so you will listen to his suggestions. A sales letter has to involve you in the imagery of living the dream or avoiding the pain.

Action. A hypnotist will give you command suggestions to do something. A sales letter has to make a call to action. It's going to ask you to fill out the order form, click here, make the phone call, go visit—whatever it happens to be.

Those parallels should make you understand that when I came up with hypnotic writing, it wasn't just a catchy title. There was some research behind it. I was fascinated by two worlds: first, the world of literature, with Jack London, Mark Twain, Shirley Jackson, and other literary giants. I used to wonder how they used the same language that's available to you and me to put us into trance states where we feel fear or anger or excitement. They did it with the same words we have.

The other part of my interest had to do with John Caples and Robert Collier and other great copywriters. How did they use the same words that we use and cause us to part with our money? That fascinated me, especially people like Collier, who did it during the Great Depression, when people were supposedly broke. They found money and send it to him because of a sales letter. Robert Collier wrote what is probably the most influential copywriting book in history: *The Robert Collier Letter Book*. That book changed my life as a writer. I was a pretty good writer before it. I was a hypnotic writer after it. That was the turning point for me. Read the sales letters in it. Get a sense for how he got into people's heads, how he merged with them, how he got them to want to buy that product or service.

In this book, Robert Collier said, "The mind thinks in pictures. One good illustration is worth a thousand words. One clear picture built up in the reader's mind by your words is worth a thousand drawings, for the reader colors that picture with his own imagination, which is more potent than all the brushes of the world's artists." Very powerful, insightful observation. That is a clue on how to write hypnotic copywriting.

P. T. Barnum also influenced me. In fact, I wrote a book about him called *There's a Customer Born Every Minute*. He was a hypnotist. He was a storyteller. He was a marketer. He was a genius. He shared what excited him. He had eyes, but saw things that other people didn't see.

One example is the little boy named Charles Stratton. Charles Stratton was known as a deformed child because he looked fine, but he was extremely short, and he wasn't growing. Everybody talked about him: "Isn't that curious?" P. T. Barnum looked at him, saw General Tom Thumb, and made him famous. He made the little guy a millionaire. He saw something different.

One year I bought 600 units of something called a massage pen. You can write with it on one end, and it vibrates on the other. If you have a headache, you might rub it against your temple. If your arm hurts, you might press the vibrating part against your arm. You can even use it on acupressure points, if you know what those are. It does relieve stress, and it's a nice conversational piece.

How would you describe a massage pen? If Joe Vitale just gave you this massage pen and someone asked, "What is that?" what would you say? A pen that relaxes you? A pen that makes you laugh? One website wrote that it was the unique metal ballpoint pen with rugged metal construction, attractive design, patented massage function, replaceable ink refills, batteries included. Is that hypnotic? It's technical. An engineer would like it. An engineer probably wrote it.

Stupid.com, a website for funny gifts, wrote, "Imagine you had a teensy-weensy masseuse to carry around in your shirt pocket. Any time you desired, you could order your mini-masseuse to soothe your tired muscles and rub away your tensions. Now imagine this tiny masseuse had a pin sticking out of his head and ran on batteries. Well, you're not likely to come across the miniature pin-headed masseuse—but there's the next best thing: the world's first massage pen!" Is this hypnotic? Yes, it's very hypnotic. It communicates the message and does it with a sense of fun.

Note the word *imagine*, which is also very hypnotic. Remember Robert Collier's remark that the mind thinks in pictures. We think in pictures, not words, or at any rate the words represent pictures. When we say *imagine*, we're actually giving a hypnotic command. You'll find this in a lot of copywriting. Sometimes people know what they're doing when they use it. Sometimes they're just copying other copywriters. (That's why we're called copywriters: because we copy.) *Imagine* is used a lot, because it's a direct command and engages your mind to start doing that very thing: you start to imagine.

Another important concept is what I call the *intimacy secret*. It's the key to hypnotic writing, but as far as I know, no copywriter has ever talked about it. Hypnotic writing makes you, the reader, feel as if you're the only person being written to.

One way to do that is to write your copy as a letter to a friend. As soon as you write it to one person, you're much more at ease, you're much more comfortable, you're much more relaxed. A lot of times, it gums up the mental works when people think, "I'm going to write a sales letter, and 100 million people are going to read it." Or "I'm going to write this book, and thousands of people will read it." Suddenly you clog up, and it becomes very difficult to communicate. You become overwhelmed with the idea of being judged by or trying to communicate with so many people.

Wipe that clean. Write the letter or the sales piece to one person. Here is the beauty of this: even if a million people read your copy, they read it one at a time. If you are using this intimacy secret and building this relationship by writing just to them, they will feel they are the only person who got the letter.

I have sent out emails to which people have replied saying, "Did you write this just to me or to everybody in your list?" They were confused because that relationship, that letter type of feeling, that personality, was there to such an extent they didn't know.

Again, at this stage of the process, forget grammar. Grammar has its place, but it's going to be at the end of the creative process. This will make more sense when I actually get to revealing my formula for writing copy, which I haven't done yet. At this point, simply forget it. You don't need to know it. Later on, you can have it reviewed by someone who does, like an editor.

Be you. This is so important, but what does it mean? Speak in your own voice, the way you would speak on the phone. Whatever examples come to you, whatever language comes to you, whatever that is for you, that's your style. That's what makes you unique, and people want to read something from somebody unique. They want to read the personality.

My colleague Pat O'Bryan wrote this copy:

Do you suffer from negative self-thought, limiting belief, lack of focus, lack of confidence? Now here's a solution. Now you can replace negative self-thought and limiting beliefs automatically, with no effort on your part. Imagine this: you sit in a comfortable position, slip on your headphones, listen for twelve or fifteen minutes, and immediately you are energized, focused, and relaxed as you listen. As you listen, affirmations based on the millionaire-making work of Napoleon Hill are effortlessly injected directly into your subconscious mind.

Again, note the word "imagine." This presupposes that the recipient is going to listen. It's a hypnotic command. It's also full of promises, and there's engagement. "Do you suffer from negative self-thought?" I want them to say yes in their head. Limiting beliefs? Yes. Lack of focus? Yes. Lack of confidence? Yes. This is an old principle of selling: you want to get them into a *yes* mindset.

Some copywriters argue that question headlines are not good because they stop the audience. Well, they stop the audience, but in an engaging way. They pull them into the copy. The only way a question would stop the audience is if it's a yes or no question.

I love questions, but they have to be open-ended. "Do you suffer from negative self-thought?" is not a good question headline, because somebody could say yes and stop reading, or say no and stop reading. (As this example shows, there are exceptions to every rule.) You want to add more, or you want to change the question to something more open-ended: what is a new way to remove negative self-thought? You don't know. Without reading the rest of the copy, you can't answer that question.

I'm also a big believer in titles and subtitles, which are like headlines: "the advanced formula for total success"; "a guaranteed path to getting the results you want."

The key words here: *formula* is good. We could have just said *formula*, but we went with *advanced formula*. We could have said *formula for success*; that's good, but we went with *formula for total success*. You see how we're qualifying and enlarging the benefits and promises?

Revealing is a very powerful word. It's a mind opener. *Guaranteed* is a famous word. *Getting results*: we could have just said *getting results* but *getting the results you want*. There was some intention in how we crafted that. Each of those words makes it so that the only choice you have is to read on. The only way to satisfy your curiosity about each one of those things is to actually read the copy. Again, I'm playing on curiosity.

I wrote a book called *The Greatest Money-Making Secret in History*. This is a book about giving, about tithing. I could have called it *Giving and Tithing: New Information*. From a hypnotic writing standpoint, that seems pretty lame to me. I fished for the best thing I could come up with: it was *The Greatest Money-Making Secret in History*. I am so proud of this title that I sometimes strut around my house. The title, written from an engaging, curiosity provoking standpoint, is better than the book.

The Greatest Money-Making Secret in History—don't you want to know? When you see the title, you ask "What *is* the greatest money-making secret in history?" That was my way of getting the most minds to be interested in that book.

I purposely added "in history" because if I had simply written, "The greatest money-making secret," some people might think it had to do with real estate or something like that. If I write, "in history," they'll think, "Well, maybe it isn't real estate; maybe it's something else that I don't know about. If it's the greatest secret in history, maybe I've overlooked it." This title raises all kinds of questions.

These titles are all on my website, MrFire.com: *The Unspoken Secret to Achieving Big Goals*, *The Real Winner of the Super Bowl*, *What E-books Will Sell This Year*. I don't ask, "Will e-books sell this year?" You can say yes or no and forget it. But if I say, "*What* e-books will sell this year?" and if you're at all interested in e-books (and even if you're not), you're probably going to wonder, "What does he think will sell this year? Does he know?"

Here's a small but important piece of information: the public soaks up prediction articles, not just at the end of the year, when we're making predictions for the new year. "What e-books will sell this year?" is a prediction. Nobody cares if you're right. Nobody goes back three months later and checks. It says, "Oh, Joe was wrong about those e-books. He mentioned ten that would sell, and only two or nine sold."

This is a great way to write a piece of copy. You can write it as a mind-engaging statement: "What will happen in the next few months?" Just fill in the blanks related to your product or service.

Another thing: built into the prediction is an implication of inherent credibility: you are an expert. That's an unspoken element built into *What E-books Will Sell This Year?*

If someone asks, "How do you know all these things are going to come true?" I will reply, "I don't know." I'll take my best shot at it, but nobody knows. That's the beauty of writing these predictions: it engages everybody, because nobody knows.

The Seven Principles of Hypnotic Writing

In his book *Breakthrough Advertising*, Eugene Schwartz wrote that a copywriter's first qualifications are imagination and enthusiasm. You are the scriptwriter for your prospect's dreams. You are the chronicler of his future. Your job is to show him in minute detail all the tomorrows that your product makes possible for him. That is another million-dollar insight on how to write hypnotic copy.

Let me go into the seven principles of hypnotic writing.

1. Make it **personal**. Hypnotic writing speaks to you. Use words such as *you, me, I,* and *your.* All of these make you feel that the writing is speaking to you personally. In fact, the more personal the writing, the more hypnotic it is. This ties into the intimacy factor I was talking about earlier.

2. Hypnotic writing is **active**. You'll use lots of verbs, with only a few passive constructions. This is a real key to hypnotic writing. It's the difference between saying, "The writing was hypnotic" and saying, "Joe Vitale weaves hypnotic writing." The first is passive; the latter is active. That's one key right there: go through an existing piece of writing, and change it from passive to active. You will make it much more engaging, much more hypnotic.

3. Hypnotic writing is **emotional**. It taps your emotions. You can use a story format (my favorite) or direct narrative: either way, the writing will pull at your heartstrings. One of my most famous letters began, "I was nearly in tears." That line engaged the emotions of readers. You feel what you're trying to express while you're writing the copy, so that when the readers read it, they can be in that same feeling modality.

4. Hypnotic writing is **sensual**. It involves your senses. You'll find descriptions of feeling, tasting, seeing, smelling, hearing. All of these will help the reader become involved with the writing and therefore susceptible to what it commands. Far too much writing out there is governmentlike or legalese. There's no person speaking to your senses. You want to speak to more than just the brain. Talk about what people will feel, what they will touch, what they will smell, what they will see. Involve all the senses in your writing.

5. Hypnotic writing is **commanding**. It commands you to do something. You may not always detect the command, as it may be embedded, but there will always be one. Ask yourself, "What do I want to do after reading this?" What you do next may be a result of a hypnotic command.

6. Hypnotic writing plays on your **curiosity**. You may begin the story at the beginning of your copy, but leave the ending till the end (one of my favorite things to do). You may tell how to do something but only give limited details, thereby urging the reader to order the book, which contains more information.

   Again, this goes back to opening the mind but not closing it until you're finished with your message.

7. Hypnotic writing is **hidden**. You won't find any obvious clues that gives the signal "Hypnotic writing at work." Instead the writing will instead be smooth and personal, and the hypnotic aspect will sneak in below conscious awareness. Today a lot of copywriters are very heavy-handed in trying to write what they think is hypnotic copywriting. For example, they'll start by saying, "Imagine," and then they'll go on with a long run-on sentence that include all of the senses. That writing's not hidden. It's too obvious. People aren't going into a trance, because they're caught up in the awkwardness of the writing. Hypnotic writing is usually hidden.

How to Learn Hypnotic Writing

Here are some ways to learn hypnotic writing that are fun. You could study great ads and sales letters. Get some books on the subject, such as Denison Hatch, whose *Million Dollar Mailings* has some of the greatest sales letters ever written. Yanik Silver has a collection of Internet pitches online. Study great ads and great sales letters. Study the headlines in the tabloids, one of the greatest places to find engaging headlines. Study the titles in *Reader's Digest*. For decades, *Reader's Digest* has been known to come up with engaging titles to make you want to read their articles. They put those titles right on the front page of the magazine, because they know you're going to glance at that. You never noticed that it's 90 percent copy. It's all words.

Study old comic book ads. They use some of the persuasion principles and structures of hypnotic writing that make this so clear for you that you're going to feel all you have to do now is fill in the blanks.

Watch what makes this work: *"Exciting ant farm. Now, for your very own, an ant's entire world, complete with stock of live ants. What is an ant farm? Fascinating, educational, world's tiniest engineers."*

Why does this work? What jumps out? "Exciting ant farm." "Exciting" is a very powerful word in itself. Then in each of the subheads, there is a benefit, and it's an emotion of its own: "Fascinating, educational. World's tiniest engineers. Seeing your tiny pets."

The ad is written for a dual audience. In the first place, they're getting the kids. "To see your tiny pets" is a big thing for a kid. Kids will often sit down on the ground and watch insects. Then "educational" and "world's tiniest engineers." That's for parents. "Educational" is not for the kid. The kid doesn't care. The kids are not buying it; the parents are.

Other features: this ad says, "Order now." There's a command there. You definitely want to include a command. Far too much copy out there doesn't tell anybody to do anything.

Furthermore, there's a coupon in this ad. All of the greatest copywriters have a direct response mechanism of some sort. Coupons attract attention. Almost all of us have been trained to look for a coupon. That means there's a deal of some sort, or the summation of the offer is in that order form. In our emails, there's a link to click on. Finally, there is an upsale in the ant farm ad. You can add another ant farm for a total cost of $6.95. You're going to have an ant empire for $7.

This product also illustrates the concept of reframing, which I mentioned in regard to P. T. Barnum and General Tom Thumb. Seeing ants, which are pests which we don't like, and selling them to people as pets—that's really reframing something.

Ants build stuff that is cool, that is fun to look at. It's underground, which is always fascinating. That's taking the positive that's inherent in the negative and flipping it around. They dig holes inside your house, but they do it in the sand in a little box, and you can see it.

It's important to make things fun. Entertainment is its own justification. People don't justify entertainment. If they want to feel entertained, that's the priority. They'll prioritize that over things that they have to do. If your product or marketing is fun, it gets around the rational, critical mind, because it has its own value. It distracts them from the mundane and boring and stressful.

Another famous ad: "*The insult that made a man out of Mac.*" This is a Charles Atlas ad for physical development. It's in comic form. A bully kicks sand in the face of a weakling and his girl at the beach. The weakling says, "*Darn it! I'm sick of being a scarecrow! Charles Atlas says he can give me a real body. All right! I'll gamble a stamp and get his free book!*" In the last panel, he looks in the mirror and says, "*Boy! It didn't take Atlas very long to do this for me! What muscles! That bully won't shove me around again!*"—very famous. At the bottom is a coupon: "*Let me prove I can make you a new man.*" That's a pretty powerful statement right there.

Milton Erickson was one of the most famous hypnotherapists of all time. Once he had to write a very difficult and confusing article. He wasn't sure how to communicate this complicated new material. He put himself into a light trance and told himself, "When I awaken, I want to have a solution to how I should write my article." When he woke up, he found comic books on his lap. He looked at them and said, "What do these have to do with my article?" He realized that he needed to write his article with the same simplicity as a comic book. It needed to have a little bit of dialogue, a little story going on, a simple message that was being communicated. And he wrote this article keeping in mind that he wanted to write it with the simplicity of a comic book. Stories are hypnotic.

I've been told that 40 percent of the publishing in Japan is comic books. Supposedly the government has published the military budget in comic form. And traffic is so bad over there that people read comics in the car. Companies do their employment manuals and safety manuals for professional people as comic books. All kinds of information are communicated that way. There are also social events. People have clubs for their comic book heroes; they have parties where they dress up. There's a whole fantasy thing about it.

It ties back to Milton Erickson simplifying everything, even for his sophisticated audience, by having a comic in mind as he did his writing. He didn't turn his article into a comic book, but he had that mindset for simplicity. It might be worth testing to put up some websites that are comic books. Use some cartoons with some dialogue and a little story.

Another thing to consider is that at least in our culture, those of us who have read comic books probably did so at a younger age. So that format may take you back to your core desires and more childlike, emotionally driven decisions: "I don't need to make the cable bill payment this month. I'm going to buy this thing because it's fun." Moreover, people are working you know so much that there is a sense of "Poor me. Hey, I deserve this because it's fun. Who cares about the logic of it?"

Yet another consideration: many people today are dyslexic or borderline dyslexic, so reading straight text is difficult for them. If there are more pictures, they will pick up on the ad more easily.

Simplicity rules.

The Atlas ad also shows that pain and pleasure are the two kinds of motivation. People go away from the pain or towards the pleasure. In this case, it's the pain of humiliation. Another ad has the headline *"Never look short again! Now you can be taller instantly!"* This ad has a lot of copy, direct response, and illustrations to show you what's going on. There are subheads throughout: *"Invite romance and be admired and respected by the opposite sex."* *"Earn more money—being taller helps you find and qualify for the best jobs."* They were working every kind of logic they could come up with.

A similar ad for some kind of martial art: *"Shhh, it's a secret. Learn the secret powers of the deadliest killers in the Orient."* People love secrets: *"Let me tell you a secret."* It also plays toward curiosity, mentioning "men who could fight or disappear." Whoa! They can fight, and they can disappear. Very engaging here—like a comic book. I think they might be appealing to that mentality. Note also the mystical element. The ad projects mystical power.

Often much of the space in an ad is taken up by the pictures, which forces the text to be very small. Off the cuff, you would think that small text would discourage reading, but it doesn't. It just means that those who read are going to be buyers. They're investing their time and their energy when they start reading. That is hypnotic for lots of reasons.

Another ad: "*An amazing invention . . . Magic art reproducer. Draw any person in one minute. No talent! No lessons!*" This summons up a benefit that people are looking for: somebody wants to draw. I remember buying that product when I was a kid. It just gave you a shadowy outline on another piece of paper, and you drew over it. It did not make anything fantastic. You wouldn't hang up your art afterwards. But for whatever it cost, it was great.

The art reproducer headline also demonstrates the product. When you're writing copy, it's wise to demonstrate what people are going to be able to do when they have your product or service. How will their life be different? Demonstrate that through your descriptions. You don't want to just have a picture. You want a picture of somebody doing something, if at all possible, and demonstrating what you're trying to convey yourself.

Some ads have highlights in yellow. Highlighting your copy is very powerful, making it much more interactive. It also makes the copy jump—the copy that you want people to pay attention to.

Today there are three kinds of readers: *word-for-word readers*, *skimmers*, and *jumpers*. Word-for-word readers, once engaged, will read every word, which is great. There are the skimmers, who are engaged because of the headline or maybe the graphic. They scan the ad quickly: "Oh, $1.98. Oh, what do I get free? Oh, OK: we've got a coupon."

Online, we have the jumpers. They're jumping either from a website or from a clip up here to a clip down here, or they move all the way down at the very end. They're not even skimming; they're jumping pages. Today there are many jumpers, because there's so much content on the Internet that we start finding shortcuts. Jumping is one of those.

But don't assume that everybody's jumping. We've got three types of readers, and we need to write to all of them. That's why every word counts.

Highlighting can also heighten intimacy. It's like picking up a book in a used bookstore and seeing what somebody else has highlighted. Somebody has taken his yellow highlighter and said, "This is important to me," so I feel an enhanced sense of connection.

Marketer Dan Kennedy is known for sending out letters that are scribbled on all over the place, with writing in the margins and comments saying, "Look at this," or "Here's the great deal" or "Read this part first." Sometimes that messier look gets more readership than a nice, neat look, double-spaced and with justified margins.

Another fundamental principle of copywriting: you want to speak in the language of your reader. You want to use graphics. You want to use the language they're going to understand, because that's whom you are communicating to. We're trying to get an edge and become the best communicators of our message to our audience.

Hot-button words are also hypnotic. One is *free*. Others are *amazing*, *unusual*, *imagine* (as we've seen), and *secret*.

The Power of Story

Research says that we are storied beings. We make sense of the world and we remember things through the story. If we don't tell or hear a story, we tend to forget the things that have been coming to us. We have to orchestrate that loose information and glue it together enough to form a story. It doesn't mean the story is right or wrong, but it is the way for us to hold details in our memory.

A story is a great way to deliver a hypnotic message. It involves relationship, humanity, and people, and you care because it's made relevant to actual life. On some level, we're all pretty practical. If something doesn't relate in any way to life, who cares? Especially in an information overload society, a story gives you a pathway through the information where you can digest it and make it real.

In all cultures, there are archetypical stories that we all recognize. Boy meets girl, they face their challenge, they separate, they either get back together or move on in different directions.

In the early twentieth century, a Frenchman named Georges Polti wrote a book called *The Thirty-Six Dramatic Situations*, which spells out thirty-six plot lines that can show up in any story. It's worth digging up, because when you want to tell a story, you want conflict, dialogue, and resolution. What was the turning point for the character? It's almost like a miniature piece of fiction, but we're not writing fiction; we're selling something or communicating our message. We want somebody to buy our product or service. You can use these thirty-six dramatic situations to do that.

The Pitch

One educator, Hugh Rank, is a bit of an alarmist. He's worried about deception in copywriting and advertising. He created a way to decipher how ads are causing you to part with your money. He designed a formula to help make people aware of methods of persuasion and avoid getting ripped off. It's in a little book he published called *The Pitch*.

Rank's formula works. He just didn't want unethical people using it. We want to use it for ethical reasons. He says, "Look at an ad, and the first thing to ask yourself is, what attention-getting techniques are used within it? Is there anything unusual from a sensory point of view? Does the ad have motion, music, sounds, visuals, or graphics that might be leading you to go toward buying what they're selling?" He's stating it as a warning; I'm stating it as a recommendation. What's wrong with having motion, music, sounds, visuals, or graphics? They can assist your selling message.

Rank also mentions emotions. Again, this is attention-getting: associations with sex, nature, fun, pets, family. Many of the ads I mentioned earlier have these elements. Rank is saying that ads use them for negative reasons. I'm saying, use them for positive reasons—thought, humor, news stories, questions, advice, lists, displays, lead-ins, demonstrations, claims, and promises. The elements of hypnotic writing work in all kinds of advertising, copywriting, and Internet marketing. Rank is saying, beware. I'm saying, use it.

Rank recommends looking for confidence building techniques. Do you recognize the product from past repetition—the brand, the logo, the company? In other words, if you see an ad from Starbucks, you're going to recognize it. He's saying be aware that that's created a relationship with you. I'm saying be aware and create a relationship with your readers.

There are also competence words being used: *trust, safe, honest*—those are words you want to use. Also non-verbals: a smile, a soothing voice, friendly, sincere.

There was a study of Coca-Cola ads from a period of over a hundred years. The researchers looked for a common ingredient besides a Coke bottle and the name in the ad. They found that it was smiling faces. Every ad had a smiling face. Without saying it, they were communicating how great you'll feel and how happy you'll be when you drink a Coke.

Another thing to be aware of: do you know, like, or trust the endorsers? Are they authority figures? Are they expert, wise, caring, protective, or are they friend figures whom you like or would like to be on your side? In other words, Rank is saying they're using a famous actor's endorsement to get you to pay attention to the ad. Of course, you can use something like that yourself.

Interestingly, Rank is presenting himself as a critic, an outsider. Many people have gotten fame for themselves by positioning themselves as critics, because the critic goes around and analyzes, say, copywriting. They'll analyze all the copywriters, and people start to think that the critic must know copywriting. Actually, the critic may just be somebody who is negative and is ripping up all copywriters. It doesn't mean they know anything at all, but they position themselves as experts. A lot of people buy into it.

Other considerations mentioned by Rank that you can use:

Desire-stimulating techniques. You want to use desire-stimulating techniques in your hypnotic copy.

The target audience. Who is the target audience?

Basic benefits. Protection, relief, prevention, acquisition. People want these things.

Is the ad product-centered? Here are some common claims: quality, quantity, efficiency, scarcity, novelty, stability, reliability, simplicity, utility, rapidity, and safety.

Is the ad audience-centered? Does it appeal to emotions, using the association technique to link the product with things the audience already likes or desires? Here are some common needs and desires often suggested in ads: basic needs (food, activity, surroundings, sex, health, security, economy); certitude or approval needs (religion, science, best people, most people, average people); space or territory needs (neighborhood, nation, nature); belonging needs (intimacy, family, groups); and growth needs (esteem, play, generosity, curiosity, creativity, complacency). You want to tie into some of those in your copywriting.

What techniques are used to stress urgency? This shouldn't come as any surprise. Even the comic book ads I reviewed have a sense of urgency and a direct response mechanism. What words are used to express urgency? *Offer expires, rush, now, deadline, last chance, one day only.* You find that all the time. You want to use something like that.

Nonverbals: staccato sounds, quick tempos in music, countdowns. What if you have a ticking clock on your website? "If you buy this before the clock hits 3:00, you get it at $57. It's normally $97." With an actual clicking clock.

Not all ads use urgency appeal, but always check for them. I think bad ads don't use urgency. If there's no urgency appeal, the ad could be a soft-sell part of a repetitive, long-term campaign to build image over time. That's known as image advertising.

Response-seeking techniques. Finally, Rank suggests looking for response-seeking techniques. Are there specific triggering words? Triggering words are hypnotic words: *buy, choose, select, to take the first step, visit, come in, ask your doctor, call 1-800, click.* Giving a command to use the product (*drink it, taste it, experience it, enjoy it*) or to get the benefit (*get, protect, prevent, relieve*).

Aristotle's Secret

Aristotle's 2,500-year-old secret for orators is a persuasion formula that is still used.

1. The *exordium* (opening) is a shocking statement or story to get attention. There is story again; 2,500 years ago, they were using stories. Talk about anchoring it in our DNA.

2. *Narratio* (narration). You pose the problem the reader is having. When you do that, you merge with their existing trance. They are already in the mindset that says, "I have this problem." If you speak to that problem, Robert Collier says you are joining with the person. You get on the same train that they're riding.

3. *Confirmatio* (confirmation). You offer a solution to the problem, which is your product or your service.

4. *Peroratio* (concluding statement). You state the benefits, which is a call to action.

This is very similar to the classic advertising formula known as AIDA: *attention*, *interest*, *desire*, and *action*. Most of my sales-oriented writing follows along the easy path of answering these questions.

These are other important questions:

1. Are you getting attention with your opening? And are you getting appropriate attention? Because you can't get attention in such a way that funnels in a whole mass of people to look at your website or read your sales letter. If they're not interested in it, they're not going to keep reading. You need to focus on a target audience.

2. Are you stating a problem the reader cares about? This goes back to targeting and to the three steps I mentioned earlier. As I've said, the list and the offer are more important than the copy.

3. Are you offering a solution that really works? This is a matter of integrity: it has to work for this particular audience.

4. Are you asking the reader to take action? I sometimes feel silly having to remind people about this, but I look at ads all the time and find this step missing. Once I saw a product that Sony was selling. I really wanted it, but there was no website, phone number, fax number, or email. There was no way to get it. Where was it? They messed up.

5. Most copywriting advice suggests that you focus on the somebody's pain. This works. You can do that. Personally, I have a no-pain formula. For what I'll call idealistic or noble reasons, I'd rather not focus on pain. I'd rather focus on pleasure.

6. I say, begin with your promise. The promise can be positive: "You can double or triple your traffic using this technology." That promise is focused on pleasure, not pain.

7. Offer proof. You can have a quote that says, "I tried this technique for the first time, and my web traffic doubled or tripled."

8. Then we have testimonials.

9. Of course, the price. We're telling them how much it is; we're making the offer.

10. The buying trance formula. This goes back to the idea that people are already in a hypnotic trance. We are

all in a mental mindset of one form or another, and we're all looking at this world differently. There's a book called *The Power of Impossible Thinking*. It talks about our mindsets, which lock us into a particular way of viewing the world. We're in a mental mindset trance.

What do your prospects believe right now? They might believe that it's possible to double or triple their web traffic, but they don't know how. If we said that you can multiply your traffic six or seven times, we probably would cross the line. They would not believe us, and they would be pulled out of the trance. But if they believe it's possible to double or triple their traffic, you point out that they don't know how. Your marketing is going to show them how.

This leads into the second part: agree with the audience's beliefs. You walk in and agree with all of those things right there. Yes, it is difficult to do this. Yes, you do need to do such and such. Take them from there to the next thing: lay your offer into their beliefs. You agree with their beliefs, then you lead into the beliefs surrounding your offer: "Yes, there is a lot of crap out there. Yes, there are a lot of people misleading you. Yes, there is a lot of hype. Yes, you can lose your money. But here's what I've been doing; here's what's true, and here's why it's true." You tell your story.

What does your audience believe right now? Of course, you can guess at that if you are part of the market and have a sense of it. You can also run a survey to get a sense of what they're thinking, or you can test. You can try different offers to find out. But after you find out what those beliefs are, you agree with them. You start where they're already at; from there, lead them to your offer, to where you want them to go.

When we use hypnotic tools in a marketing arena, everybody in that arena is for the most part already using those tools. They all know about the power of a sales letter. They've read the books out there. But as soon as you step out of the marketing arena into your specific arena, they don't know anything about marketing techniques. You're offering a breath of fresh air to them; it's much more engaging, much more riveting. Responses are tremendously higher, because nobody else is using this kind of heavy-duty gunpowder to go in there and make the case. That's the good news for all of us.

A lot of copywriters and marketing people copy what they think is working, but because they don't know the logic behind it, they don't know the psychology to make it work. They're clumsy at it, and it's not working. They're shooting themselves in the foot.

A lot of people do learn some of the basics of marketing but don't implement it very well. It's important to be clear within yourself. Some marketers think, "I should

write a sales letter. I should have a call to action." But
their call to action is either missing or incredibly weak
Something within them wasn't clear about their product,
so they didn't put it in. They end up saying, "Marketing
on the Internet doesn't work," or "Sales letters don't work."
They'll blame it on everything but refuse to look in the
mirror.

Some people have a fear of the money that's involved
in the transaction. If that's where their current trances
are at, you want to meet them there and guide them to
wherever you want them to go. You can build rapport and
trust by meeting them, not by hitting head-on, arguing
with them, or saying they're wrong. Instead you say, "I
believe the same thing," or "I used to believe that." There's
a way to meet them in their existing trance. Agree with it.
Then take it from there to where you want to go.

I also believe in using the language that your audience is used to. You're not going to speak in a different
language to them. You're one of them, speaking to them.

Dan Kennedy has said that he's tired of hearing the
number one excuse he hears from people for not imple-
menting the techniques he teaches: "It will not work in
my market or for my audience." That's what he hears all
the time. But when marketers use the techniques appro-
priately and correctly, they do work.

One example was a corporate attorney who was dealing with other corporate attorneys. His first impulse was

to say that they were not going to respond to screaming-headline direct mail twelve pages long. Dan said, "Try it." They responded. They are people. They want a story, and they want to buy solutions to their problems.

Joe's Three Big Secrets

Let me share some secrets that I haven't talked about anywhere else before.

SET AN INTENTION

The first is, I don't do all the writing. I am a great believer in directing the mind to create the results I want. When I have something to write, I don't immediately sit down and start typing. Sometimes that happens, but not all the time. Usually I give myself a mental command: "I want to write a sales letter for such and such product, and I really need it by Thursday. Work on it, and when it's time for me to start writing, nudge me, and I promise that I will stop whatever I'm doing and start writing."

I usually even make it more specific: "I want to write a sales letter that's going to get a 90 percent response" or something that I believe is potentially possible. I won't say 100 percent, because that's going past my point of belief at this moment, but I might say 90 percent. I tell myself, "Cook on it. Let it incubate. If you need me to do something, tell me."

In short, I set an intention. There is real magic here. If for some reason you don't want to hear about magic or metaphysics, look at it from a psychological standpoint. Whatever you focus on expands. You're focusing your entire mind and all of your energy on creating a sales letter that's going to get a particular response.

As I've said, your brain is an answer-seeking, radar-detecting problem solver. So you want to give it a task.

Of course, I've also fed my mind. I've researched the product, read about it, and used it. (I'll say more about this in the next chapter.) I've fed my mind. Once I've fed my mind with this research, I turn the job over. I've released it to my subconscious. One or two times, I was driving on the freeway at seventy-seven miles an hour, and a nudge started to come up. Well, I made an agreement, so I pulled over and started writing.

DIALOGUE WITH YOUR MIND

As far as I know, no other copywriter does this, so it's a little bit of an edge. At this point, I've written my draft. As I reread it, I have dialogue in my mind: What are the readers thinking as they read this? What are they questioning? What are they wondering? Is this clear? I'm looking for any objections they may have. I'm guessing at most of this, because I can't really know, but I'm tuned in as intuitively and intellectually as I can be to communicating to this audience. I'm asking what's going on in their head as they're reading. I'm dialoguing with myself to guess their objections, their confusions, and where they need clarity. Then I rewrite the relevant parts.

WRITE AND REWRITE

The third secret: I plug in hypnotic language later. All the great writers are great rewriters. Ray Bradbury did this all of his life. Not knowing what he was going to say, he would sit down and write a short story. Later, he would rewrite it. Often it was garbage. Often it was a classic of literature.

In the rewriting stage, you go through and fine-tune your material. You plug in the missing pieces. You use elements of hypnotic writing, thinking, "Oh, that's a good place for me to put in this phrase." Imagine what it would be like, and add it to what you've already written.

These three priceless secrets have enabled me to accomplish the writing I've done. I've often been asked, "How have you cranked out so much work?" Most of the time, it's because when I write something, it came to me. I honored it and wrote it in a rush. This doesn't have to do with speed: the enthusiasm and excitement forced me to get it all on paper.

Then I quickly go through, asking, what do the readers need to know next? What are their objections? Where do they need clarification? I put that in there. Third, I plug in hypnotic language, adding some points and clarifiers.

Then a fourth tip: I let someone, perhaps an editor, go through the draft and tell me what doesn't make sense. I find out where I have I missed the mark and where I haven't been grammatically correct. I let the editor fine-tune the writing, but the whole process is very quick. As Dan Kennedy says, "Money likes speed."

3

How I Write Copy

Let me tell you about my specific way of writing copy.
We all know the importance of having a headline. I start with the headline. I find that I can't write the copy without it. It anchors and sums up, in an almost telegraphic way, what I'm trying to convey. It's a working headline. When I'm done with the actual copy, I may come up with something different, but I need a headline to begin with. This is one of Joe's secrets to writing copy.

I come up with the headline by researching the product. I need to be intimate with the product. Whenever somebody says, "Will you give an endorsement for something?" I always tell them, "You've got to send it to me. I have to try it. If I like it, I'll look into giving an endorsement." It's the same thing for writing a sales letter. I can't write a sales letter for something I'm not familiar with. The research comes first. Then I look for the excitement out of the research.

Other copywriters might say they're looking for the product's uniqueness, and that's another way of saying it, but I look for the excitement. What is exciting about this product or service? What makes it different? What makes it unique? Why should the target audience jump up and down and be excited about it? I need to know what that is because my last name, Vitale, means *life* in Italian: vitality. That's how I write my copy. I look for the thing to be enthused about. That's what I'm going to focus on, and that's what I want to communicate.

I always ask to see the product or service. Make some notes pertaining to the intention you've set. What do you know about your product or service? Maybe some highlights, maybe some facts, maybe some benefits, maybe some things that you want to get across in the copy.

One of the most famous examples of doing research is David Ogilvy, the famous ad man, who was assigned to write copy for an ad for Rolls-Royce. He went through the technical manuals, and he found a line buried there. It became the headline for his ad: "At sixty miles an hour, the loudest noise you'll hear in this new Rolls-Royce is the ticking of the clock." He didn't even have to think of the line. He spotted it.

I asked Dan Kennedy about coming up with material, and he said the same thing. Sometimes you meet with clients, you listen to them, and they tell you what the copy is. Do this in conversation. If you ask them, "Write that down. You're doing great; write it up," they'll freeze. They'll suddenly be unable to express themselves. Let them relax and give them a glass of wine or something, or just say, "Tell me: why did you get in the business?" or "What do you like about your product?" They'll tell you conversationally what they love. In that conversation, you'll find gems that are much like that technical piece of material that David Ogilvy found.

Once I know what's unique and exciting about the product, I need a headline. How am I going to come up with headlines?

I researched that for *The AMA Complete Guide to Small Business Advertising* that I wrote for the American Marketing Association. I researched all of the marketing and advertising techniques to the last 150 years, looking for the similarities, for what always worked. I ended up with thirty different types of headlines. I wrote that book for myself: that way, every time I have to write something, I don't have to go back through 150 years of materials. I narrowed it all down to the thirty things that work. Here they are:

1. Lead with these opening words:

At Last!

Announcing!

New!

Note the hint of excitement and news in the above words. Other good opening words include *introducing* and *finally*. Legally you can only use the word *new* if your product has been developed or improved within the last six months. If you have just invented a new device, certainly let the world know.

2. Round up your audience.

Plumbers!

Housewives!

Sore Feet?

This type of headline calls in your target audience. If you are selling a book for lawyers, you might open by saying "Attention lawyers!" With this approach, you are certain to get the ear of the exact crowd you want.

3. Promise a benefit.

Free from Backache in 10 Minutes!

Buy One Shirt—Get the Second FREE!

Land a Job in 2 Days with New Method!

Benefits are why people buy. Decaffeinated coffee is a feature; "lets you sleep better" is a benefit. If people have a back problem, they do not want to buy a pill; they want to buy relief from their pain. *"Free from backache in 10 minutes"* tells them a cure is available. Sell the relief, not the prevention.

4. Make it newsworthy.

> *Major Breakthrough in Car Safety*
> *New Formula Restores Hair*
> *Seven "Lost Secrets" Discovered*

People devour news. Reveal the newsworthiness of your product or service, and you will get attention. A new product is news. An old product with new uses is news. Arm & Hammer baking soda has been around for decades, but the company keeps thinking of new ways for us to use its product—from brushing our teeth to putting it in the fridge to eliminate odors—and *that's* news.

5. Offer something free.

> *FREE to Writers!*
> *FREE Report Explains Tax Loopholes*
> *FREE Book on Car Repairs*

Your free item has to be appropriate to the audience you are after. It may be free, but if they are not interested in it, they will not write or call you. Also, your free item has to be *really* free—with no catches or conditions—for you to be legally safe. Any small business can create a free item that is relevant.

6. Ask an intriguing question.

What Are the Seven Secrets to Success?

Do You Make These Mistakes in English?

Which Gas Filter Will Boost Your Car's Performance?

Questions are a powerful way to involve readers. But your question has to be open-ended, and it has to hint of a benefit. If you ask a question that can be easily answered with a yes or no, you run the risk that your readers will not look beyond the question. But if your question is intriguing, it will pull them into your copy to learn the answer.

7. Lead with a testimonial.

"This is the most powerful weapon I've ever seen!"

—Clint Eastwood

"These two books made me the wealthiest man alive."

—Malcolm Forbes

"Here's why my race cars beat all others."

—Mark Weisser

There is something about quotation marks that captures people's eyes. If your quote is intriguing (like the fictional ones above), they will force readers to read your copy. (Always use real testimonials from real people, and always get their permission first.) Anyone who has ever used your product or service can give you a testimonial. Headlines put in quotes will get more attention. Dialogue has life, and that attracts people.

8. Create a "how-to" headline.

How to Get Your Kids to Listen

How to Tell When Your Car Needs a Tune-up

How to Win Friends and Influence People

Because people want information, they are easily drawn to how-to headlines that promise a benefit they are interested in. If you are selling washing machines, you might conjure up the headline *"How to pick the right washing machine for your needs."* You can add sparkle to virtually any headline by adding the word "how." *"I cut hair"* is a weak headline, but *"How I cut hair"* is more interesting.

9. Quiz your readers.

How Smart Are You? Take This Quiz and See!

What Is Your Networking IQ?

Are You Qualified for Success?

People love quizzes. Use a question headline, and then let the body of your ad be a quiz. For the ad to work, of course, it all has to tie in to what you are selling. The ad about your networking IQ, for example, is selling a book called *Power Networking*. If your ad is for a mechanic's shop, you might ask, *"Is your car healthy? Take this quiz and see!"* Your whole attempt is to somehow *involve* readers with your ad. A quiz is one way to do that.

10. Use the words "these" and "why" in your headline.

These Boats Never Sink

Why Our Dogs Cost More

Why These Skis Are Called "Perfect"

When you use the words "these" and "why" in your headline, you tend to create an attention-grabbing statement that will draw readers into the rest of your ad. If you just said, "Our skis are perfect," few would be interested. But when you say, "*Why* these skis are called perfect," you generate curiosity—one of the most powerful motivators around. Simply add the word "why" to an existing headline to make it more engaging.

"*Buy plumbing supplies here*" is boring, but "*Why people buy plumbing supplies here*" is interesting.

11. Use "I" and "me" headlines.

They Laughed When I Sat Down at the Piano—But When I Started to Play!

I Finally Discovered the Secret to Easy Writing!

Everywhere I Stick My Nose, I Make Money

First-person headlines will work if they generate enough curiosity and hold out a benefit. Everyone interested in playing the piano will be drawn to the first headline (one of the most successful in history). "You" and "yours" in a headline do not always work, because they signal a selling message, and people can become defensive. But "I" and "me" in a headline can deliver a selling message in a palatable way. Here's a good example: *"I wanted to help people, so here's why I opened my own insurance agency!"*

12. Put your product name in your headline.

How Gymco Vitamins Make Runners Lightning-Fast
The Fiskin Ladder Saved My Husband's Life
Thoughtline Helped Me Discover the Secret to Easy Writing

"How to cure warts" is good, but *"How Vitalist cures warts"* is better. Since not everyone will stop and read your ad, putting your company name in the headline helps deliver some of your message. But do not make your company name the *focus* of your headline. Instead, write a riveting headline and slip your name in it.

13. Use the word "wanted."

Wanted—Nervous People
Wanted—Safe Men for Dangerous Times
Wanted—Executives Ready for Sudden Profits

"Wanted" is a word loaded with curiosity. Lead with it, and people will feel compelled to find out why you want nervous people (maybe for a seminar on overcoming fear) or why you want executives (maybe to offer them your new management program). Be sure to ask for the target audience you want.

14. Use the word "breakthrough" in your headline.

A Breakthrough in Alarm Systems

Doctor Offers Breakthrough Hair-Loss Formula

"Breakthrough" implies news. It suggests that your product or service beats all other existing systems. A similar impact can be obtained with "record-breaking" or "revolutionary."

15. Set your headline in upper and lower case.

HEADLINES IN ALL CAPS ARE HARD TO READ

Headlines in Upper and Lower Case Are Easy to Read

Got it?

16. Use as many words as you need.

It Floats!

How Often Do You Hear Yourself Saying, "No, I haven't Read It; I've Been Meaning To"?

Who Else Wants Beautiful Furniture?

Headlines can be long or short. As long as they get the attention of your audience, arouse curiosity, and encourage people to read your ad, any length goes. You do not want to waste words, of course. But you do not need to limit yourself either.

17. Feature your offer.

Arrow Shirts at 50% Off

Oil Change Special

Join for Six Months—Get Next Six Months Free

For this to work, you have to be clear about the uniqueness of what you are selling. What are you offering that is head and shoulders above your competition? Focus on that.

18. Ask "who else?"

Who Else Wants to Write a Book?

Who Else Used to Say Singing Was Hard?

Who Else Wants a Fail-Safe Burglar Alarm?

"Who else?" is an involving set of words. It suggests that someone else has what you are offering and that it is possible for the reader to have it too.

19. Use a guarantee.

Guaranteed No-Stains-Ever Rug!

Guaranteed to Go through Ice, Mud, or Snow—Or We
    Pay the Tow!

We live in the age of skepticism. Your ad should always run with a guarantee (more about that later). But if your headline says your offer is guaranteed, it will help to convince readers to look at your entire ad.

20. Admit a weakness.

We're Number Two. We Try Harder.

This Chef Makes Everything Except Salads!

You will gain credibility if you confess you are not perfect. Too many ads claim to be the magic bullet for all your ills. That is not believable. If you say you are *almost* a magic bullet, people will tend to believe the rest of your claims.

21. Focus on positive end results.

Whiter Teeth in 10 Days

35 Pounds Slimmer in 30 Days

Do not paint a negative picture thinking you will make a sale. People buy hopes and dreams. Do not sell "fat loss"; instead sell "perfect health!" Do not try to scare people into buying toothpaste by yelling "Yellow teeth are ugly." Instead, sell the end result people want: "Whiter teeth!" Again, people buy cures. But be believable. If your headline sounds like a stretch, people will not trust you: "35 pounds slimmer in 30 days" is believable; "35 pounds slimmer overnight" is not.

22. Warn your audience.

Warning to Doctors!

Warning: Do Your Kids Play This Stereo?

Small Business Owners Be Warned!

You can grab your target audience with a warning to them. It promises information and invokes curiosity.

23. Be careful with humor.

Not everyone has a sense of humor, not everyone agrees on what is funny, and few people buy because of a joke. A slogan in advertising is, "People don't buy from clowns." Small businesses that attempt to sell people with humor usually flop. Why? You are not selling humor; you are selling your product or service. Do you want people to laugh or buy? If you insist on trying humor, try to make the punch line the same as your sales message. Here is an example: "Used Car Prices So Low, It Hertz."

24. Make it easy.

Plumbing Problems Cured Easily
Easy Way to Solve Roof Leaks

People want results fast and easy. If you or your product can make their life easier, say so.

25. Be careful with reverse type.

You can use reverse type (white letters on a black background) for your headline, but *do not* use reverse type for the rest of your ad. Too much reverse type is far too difficult for people to read. Using it in a headline, however, can increase the number of people who will see the ad.

26. Dramatize the benefit.

Stop Sleeping like a Sardine! Now Sleep like a King!

"Sound Pillow" Lets You Sleep with Neil Diamond!

People want action. They crave it. Show the excitement your product or service can give by dramatizing the benefits. A headline for large beds that reads "King-size beds are roomy" is boring, but "Stop sleeping like a sardine! Now sleep like a king!" is almost impossible to ignore.

27. Use proven clichés.

JUST ARRIVED—New Accounting Method!

ADVICE to Homeowners!

THE TRUTH ABOUT Shoe Repair

David Ogilvy, in *Confessions of an Advertising Man*, lists the following as proven headline clichés: *free, new, how to, suddenly, now, announcing, introducing, it's here, just arrived, important development, improvement, amazing, sensational, remarkable, revolutionary, startling, miracle, magic, offer, quick, easy, wanted, challenge, advice to, the truth about, compare, bargain, hurry, last chance.* (For my own list, which is similar, see chapter 9.)

Ogilvy also says you can strengthen a headline by adding emotional words such as *darling, love, fear, proud, friend,* and *baby.*

28. Reveal a hidden benefit.

How to Get Enthusiastic Applause—Even a Standing Ovation—Every Time You Speak!

This headline by Ted Nicholas sold a publication for speakers. One of the hidden or side benefits of reading it is learning how to get a standing ovation—something every speaker wants. Try to reveal the hidden benefit in your business. Ask yourself, "What will people get as a result of using my product or service?"

29. Give reasons.

Three Reasons Why You Should Write a Book
Seven Reasons to Call This Doctor Today
Nine Reasons to Use This Maid Service

Reasons involve readers with your ad. To learn more, they have to read the rest of your copy. The trick to making this work is in targeting your prospects. If you are an accountant, give reasons that tie in to your service. If you are a baker, give reasons why your baked goods are better.

30. Use a before-and-after statement.

The Wrong Way and the Right Way to Buy a Used Car

This is a common way to show how your business can make a difference. If you own a gardening service, you might use a headline that suggests you transform gardens from jungles to parks. What you are doing here is comparing what people have (their problems) with what you can give them (the solution).

Unleash Your Mind

When we write, we have two parts that are fighting each other. One is trying to write and one is trying to edit. They don't work well together. So I suggest streak writing as a type of meditation. Put the editorial part aside. You can always make a deal with it. You can say, "You know what? I do need your editorial help, but not right now. I'll invite you back later, and you can have a joyful time slashing my writing all you want, but not right now."

The next step is unleashing the mind. That's when I sit down and write. There's a real key to making this work. It's going to sound simplistic, but it's incredibly power-ful: sit down and write uninterruptedly for ten minutes. These are the rules: no stopping, no editing, no pausing. If you can't think of what to stay while you're moving your pen, write, "I can't think of what to say." Whatever you're thinking, write it down. No editing.

You may find that you're questioning or critiquing yourself as you're writing: "The spelling is wrong; the punctuation is wrong." "Are you sure you know what you're doing right there?" "Shouldn't you be washing the car right now?" "Did you feed the cat?" This what goes in our head as we write. It's all garbage. Be aware of it, and go on writing anyway.

I once gave an exercise like this to people in a workshop. I turned on the clock and said, "Go ahead and write for ten minutes. Just write out whatever you want." I didn't give them any other directions. I sat there for ten minutes sweating, because I thought, "Are they going to get it?" I couldn't tell by looking at their faces, which were blank. Were they excited? Were they bored? Did they think I was nuts? What were they writing?

Some were writing furiously, and some were stopping. At the end of the ten minutes, I reluctantly said, "OK. Do you want to tell me what happened?"

My God, the breakthroughs! One woman was in tears. She said, "I have not written this much or this well in years." One man, a therapist, had already finished his book and turned it in to the publisher. He said, "I have to get to a phone. I got to get my book back from the publisher. I just wrote a whole new foreword because of what I learned from your hypnotic writing techniques. I have to rewrite the book."

One guy had been sitting there. He had stopped writing, and I was ready to criticize him a little. He said, "I wrote a whole new story that's going to go into my collection." He lifted it up and showed me how much he had written. All of these people had breakthroughs. It was fantastic.

Years ago, I taught people to do this free-form writing—basically trusting themselves. Some people ended up writing books. One woman had not written a word, not a letter, since she was in high school, because she had gone home with a bad grade on one of her papers, and her father ripped her up over it. He really upset her. It was an emotional trauma. She did not write again until she learned to let go of that critical part of her.

Here's another technique I use at this stage. After you've set your intention and you're ready to write, turn on your computer and set up your document. Then turn off the monitor and start writing.

It's weird to start with, because it dislocates the editorial part of your mind, which says, "What am I writing? What did I just say?" The beauty of this practice is that as you keep going through it, creativity starts coming out, as long as you forget the critical, editorial part of the mind. When you're all done, turn the monitor back on, and all of what you've written is back.

You'll be surprised, because studies show that creativity improves—including spelling, punctuation, and grammar. Somehow the writing comes naturally from the source that already knows what it's supposed to be like. You'll probably still have to do some fine-tuning; I always have to. As I said earlier, there are no great writers; they're all great rewriters. But in this part of the process, you're writing a first draft as fast as you can to get the essence down, to get the creative spark down, knowing that you can look at it and critique it later.

I want you to experience this approach to writing. Try it right now. Get some writing materials, and set your clock or smartphone to ring in ten minutes.

Start writing. Remember the ground rules: Don't stop. Write whatever you want, but keep in mind your intention and your research, and write in that direction.

You're not going to share your writing with anybody. You're not going to put it on a website. No one is going to look at it and make fun of you.

Keep the pen moving. If you don't know what to say, write, "I don't know what to say." Don't worry about checking facts. Check facts later.

When the alarm rings, write a few keywords to remind you of where you want to go when you pick it up later.

This exercise may take a little practice. You may have started editing, but once you realize that this is the inner editor, you understand that you have a choice of listening to it or not. You are in control. You can even yell at this inner voice and tell it to shut up: "Come back another time. I'll invite you back. You're going to have your time to come play, but not right now."

Awareness is crucial. I treat writing, even copy-writing, as a type of meditation. I've realized you are sep-arate from that editorial voice. It is not you; it was planted there, possibly by your father or some other authority figure, and groomed overtime. It may also involve a collection of fears of exposure to other people's criticism. You can choose to listen to it and say, "OK. You want me to edit right now, but I'm not going to listen to you," and keep writing.

In 1964, Eric Berne published a best-selling book called *Games People Play*. It talked about a way of looking at personality called *transactional analysis*. By this theory, each of us has a parent, adult, and child inside. Essentially, the child is a free, hugely creative, absolutely unfettered, pure being. Then there is the parent, which we've inherited from our own parents. They passed on to us the anxieties and conflicts that they got from their own parents, along with a desire to protect us, so they were constantly trying to civilize us and rein us in. We've internalized that process, and we're doing that to ourselves. We're always pulling ourselves in. It's important to develop the part that's called the adult—the part that can remember not to do inappropriate things in public or cross the street without looking. But when you're writing your first draft, it's OK to get back into that little kid and honor it.

The more permission we give ourselves to move around these parts, the freer we become. In the center of all of this inner activity is you. You want to be in the center of the cyclone. Let these thoughts and voices swirl around and go into orbit, or invite them back.

There is a positive reason for having the editorial voice.

Most of the time it's trying to protect you; it's trying to make you look good. You're going to write something that's going on a website; you're a big shot; you're a famous master list builder; you've got to look good. But at this stage, be as free as you possibly can. Be that center of the storm, because you're going to rewrite in the next stage. In fact, your rewrites will be a lot easier, because what you're rewriting will be so much better.

Now let me explain how to rewrite your copy. I use Stephen King's advice. Make ten copies of your writing and hand them to ten peers (not family members, because most of the time, they will use it as an excuse to criticize you, not just your work). When their feedback comes in, look for the majority votes. If one or two say, "I don't like the headline," or "I don't like the particular subject," or "Something doesn't make sense," take a look at it, of course. But if all of them say, "Boy, this first page should be in the last page, and this headline should be not on the page at all, and maybe this page three topic should be the headline," you'd better change it or at least take a very hard, close look at it.

I do this all the time with my writing. If you look at the acknowledgments in my books, you'll see at least a dozen readers listed. These were the people who saw the book before it ever went to press. They saw it off in a rough draft form and gave me advice. I went through the book with their advice in mind and rewrote it.

We are too close to our work; that's why we need somebody who's objective to look at it. You don't have to pay these ten people anything, They're glad to do it. Over time, you will learn which people will do it and which people won't. Someone may keep saying, "I'll get to it. I'll get to it." Scratch them off the list. They're not going to turn it in. The next time you write something, and you give it out to your group, that person is no longer in it. You've learned that they're not going to give you feedback.

Here's another insight: whenever you see a comma, see if you can change it to a period. People often write sentences that are far too long. Rather than using commas to set off clauses in a sentence, try using periods. Create several shorter sentences. This will make your writing move. This is one of Joe's ways of activating his writing so it's much more hypnotic. I try to use as few commas as possible. If I find a lot of commas in that first draft, I go back and say, "Can I take those commas out? Will the sentence still make sense? Or can I put a period there, stop the sentence, and start a new one to make it easier for people to read?"

Write in active language. As I've already mentioned, passive language is boring. Active language is hypnotic. It's a major secret. "The book was read by me" is passive while

"I read the book" is active. Look for the helping words *with*, *is*, *was*, *are*, or *be*. They're signals that you've written a passive sentence.

This is one of my old favorites: people say, "I can't edit my words. I can't reduce the copy." If someone said they'd pay you $1,000 for every word you took out of your letter, would you be able to take some words out? Probably. If you really thought they were going to give you a $1,000 per word you cut, you'd edit it pretty ruthlessly.

Next, rearrange paragraphs. Most great writers are word sculptors. Become a Michelangelo of words. Pretend this is a game, and the paragraphs are like chess pieces. Just move them around. Rearrange your writing to make the most sense.

Word processing software enables you to pick up blocks of words and move them. Before that, writers like me would print out our copy, cut it out into paragraphs, and move them around like pieces in a puzzle. Does this go here or does it go up here? Now, of course, we do this on a computer.

I've often had this happen: With *The Seven Lost Secrets of Success*, the last chapter was originally the first. When people read the early version of the book, they said, "This is a good book, but this first chapter really feels like it should be the last." Almost everybody said that. I yanked it out and moved it to the back. People reading it today don't have a clue that that took place.

Another thing I mentioned earlier: I practice what I call my psychic skills. I'm always wondering what will be in the reader's mind at a given point. I then address it there. That's guessing, but if you do this enough, you start to get an inner sense: "About here, they're probably wondering this." Whatever they're wondering, you probably need to address it.

Next: insert hypnotic commands. This is also one of my big secrets. I go through my draft and add, change, or rewrite current statements into truly hypnotic ones. It could be something like, "Imagine when you were back in high school, and you were looking for a cheat sheet to help you get a good grade."

Read your writing out loud. This is another major step. It can be very revealing. When you speak your words, you are forced to slow down and become more aware of them. But here's an even bigger secret. This is like a million-dollar tip: get someone to read your writing to you. It make errors or awkward parts glaringly obvious. If the person reading your writing stumbles, wrinkles their brow, or seems confused, take a note of where they are at. Fix it.

I cannot stress how enlightening it is to hand a sales letter to somebody and say, "Would you read this to me?" If they start stumbling, if they don't read it smoothly, then I have some problems with the readability of that letter. Sometimes they'll wrinkle their brow and then say,

"Oh, OK. I get it," and keep going. Otherwise you'd never have known that stumbling block was there. You want to know what that stumbling block is. If they read your letter in front of you, you can catch those parts. You may also want to have a copy of the letter in front of you so you can mark these points.

Another tip: ask yourself where someone will probably skip a section in your writing. Trust your intuition. If you sense a paragraph is boring, rewrite it, break it into smaller sections, or delete it. A famous novelist once said, "I try to leave out the parts people skip." Ask yourself, what are people going to skip in my writing? Is this getting a little boring? I'm pretty ruthless when it comes to editing. If I seriously suspect that somebody's going to skip something, I try to leave it out.

Use the checklist that I'm going to give you in chapter 7. It's a twenty-one-point checklist for going through any piece of writing. This is a famous checklist. You're going to love it.

The last thing that I do when I'm going through my process of hypnotic writing is test it. This provides feedback. Testing your ad is profoundly easy on the Internet. You put it up, you send some traffic to it, or you take out a Google ad and test it to see what's going on. You pay attention to the feedback, because that's only way to know.

There is nobody, no marketer, no copywriter, no Internet authority that knows the future results of any campaign. You've got to put it out there and find out what the reaction is going to be.

Here are some final tips to summarize the insights of this chapter. Writing is easy if you follow these steps.

- Remember to keep free of the blocks.
- Know how to shut up the inner critic.
- Set the intention and walk away. As someone once said, you don't get ideas at the computer; you get them when you're away from the computer. When I set the intention for what I want to achieve, I go about my business. When I start thinking about my intention, I'm still locked into the controlling conscious mind.
- Let the music in you take over. You may even want to listen to actual inspirational music in the background.
- Know how to tune out distractions. There's a movie with Kevin Costner called *For the Love of the Game*. He plays a baseball pitcher. In the film, when he gets out on the mound, he's got 60,000 people screaming, both friendly and angry. Then all the sound goes away. He just shuts the crowd out. If you're working at home and have screaming kids, you can use big headphones that cancel out all the noise.
- Remember the power of rewriting. It's like polishing. You come back and polish, bringing out the deeper layers that you weren't aware of initially.
- And finally, don't forget that you can draw a lot more out of your talent than you ever thought possible.

Read Your Reader's Mind

As I've said, part of my process in writing hypnotic copy is trying to guess what people are thinking or guessing, or doubting or objecting. I'm fishing for their objections and then try to answer them in my copy. It's a type of mind reading. In his copywriting seminar, Dan Kennedy says he likes to write down a list of all the reasons why somebody won't buy. Then he answers all of those reasons. He addresses all of them.

This is a perfect example. I got a sales letter from Dan once for an information seminar he was giving. He began it with "How to Get Rich." I think that's a great headline. Remember, one item on the list of thirty ways to write headlines is to write how-tos.

Then he goes on to what the average person on the street thinks of in terms of getting rich. He answers with the problems with these. What's the first? The lottery. That's the first thing on his list. He's merging with the mindset of the public. Second is, marry rich. Third, inherit wealth. Fourth, steal wealth. Five, build an ordinary business. Six, join us in the info business. He takes you from where you are right to where he wants you to go.

Then he takes every one of your objections. Because this seminar costs $3,000, the first objection, is "It's too pricey for me." He answers it.

The second one is, "I want more of Dan," because Dan Kennedy is a popular speaker, but he's not doing all of the seminar. He answers the objection. He replies, "I'm going to be there. I'm going to give one of the presentations."

Then he goes on to the opposite objection: "I've had enough of Dan for now." Now he's got the other half: the ones who say, "I don't want to go to hear Dan again." He replies, "I'll only speak once."

The next objection is the location: "It's in Cleveland, for crying out loud. Who wants to go to Cleveland?" He points out that you're going there for profit, not for play.

I think this is brilliant, because I looked at it and thought, "He pretty much has wiped out every objection I have to going to this."

He even has this objection: "What can I possibly learn that I don't already know, or get that I don't already have?" That's the objection people like me might have. He answers it. You're left with the idea that you might as well sign up, because you don't have an excuse not to.

How to Get Copywriting Work

I can also give you some advice on getting copywriting work. First, I would do what I did in the beginning: read and memorize Bob Bly's books, *Secrets of a Freelance Writer* and *The Copywriter's Handbook*. Those books kick-started me as a copywriter.

There are websites where you can go to post your availability, such as Linketh and UpWork. I love the Internet because you can get both local and international clients; of course, it all depends on what you want to do. You can advertise yourself locally if you want to start with local clients.

Another good approach is to go to copywriters that are already in business and say, "Look, you probably get more work than you can handle. How about sending some my way? I'll do the first job for free." I usually ask them to do the first job for me for free. It's kind of a test, and a lot of them drop off. If they do it and do it well, I feed business to them.

Don't send samples with your initial letter. This is just a letter of introduction: "Hi, this is who I am. I understand you do copy. I've been doing copy. I've just finished Joe Vitale's *Hypnotic Selling Secrets*. I can print you samples of my work." Do not send samples first. I hate that. I don't want to see the attachments. I don't want to see anything. That's assuming I'm going to be interested, and I'm not. I've got to find out who you are and sense my own interest first. I judge people on that initial letter. I judge their writing style—not the people, but whether they can write or not.

4
How to Write Email

Email copywriting is a subset of copywriting, although it has some slightly different rules. You want to get your email opened and read immediately. You want the recipient to take action, presumably to buy something or go to an affiliate link. That is the part where you crank out cash on demand.

Email is the point of contact between you and your subscribers. It works by building a relationship that is geared towards making sales. Email copywriting is crucial to anything you're trying to do online. People either open your emails, read them, and take action, or they don't. I've found that promotions either bomb or they do really well.

Let me talk a little bit about inbox psychology. The inbox is the battleground where you're trying to gain attention and market share. Let's look at what you're competing with.

Personal email, I believe, is king. If you get a letter from your best friend or your mom, you're opening that ahead of the one from your boss. If you have valued subscriptions from an authority you like and respect, you have an existing relationship. Other marketers, of course, are like you, trying to squeeze in the door and get attention. Then of course, there's spam, which is the party pooper for everybody; it muddies up the waters.

Who's It From?

The first key element is the *name*. Who's the email from? This is very often a neglected piece, but I think it's almost as important if not more important than the subject line. If I get an email from a person I know and admire, I'm opening it. I really don't care what the subject line is.

Some newbie marketers have the urge to come up with business names like "Global MegaCorp International Limited." "Global MegaCorp" doesn't mean anything. Another is "financial"—who is that from? What is that? How many people rush to open something that says "financial"? In my world, that is a guarantee to get you deleted.

The Subject Line

The *subject line* is the equivalent of the headline. As with the headline in a sales letter, you need to put a large portion of your effort into it. It may be the only chance you'll have, beyond who the email is from, to get the recipient to open it.

You can open, for example, with a fairly standard copywriting headline: *"Do you make these massive mistakes?"* The subject line encourages the recipient to open it. Here it's a question, which, as we've seen, is hypnotic. It encourages participation and builds curiosity. If I'm writing to copywriters, they would want to know what massive email marketing mistakes would be.

What makes a good subject line? How well it actually matches up with what the recipient gets when they open the email. Some people use "Re:" in the subject line, which usually means that this is a reply. But if there was no request, it's a stupid subject line, because it completely blows any connection between the writer and the recipient. The writer is using tricks and dishonesty, so I don't care what else they're trying to tell me about. It's all done as far as I'm concerned. But I see that all the time, even from people that should know better.

Here's another one that I got: "How did it go on Monday?" This looks as if you really know the person, but it was just a bunch of Viagra prices. Another variant: "Your appointment." These often carry viruses too.

Another subject line I got was just stupid: "Health and pharmacy." Even if it weren't spam, is there any implied benefit or anything at all going on with that? No. There's nothing in it for me. In short, there needs to be a synergy between your subject line, the "from," and what you deliver.

The Body of the Email

I always begin the body of the email with "Hi" followed by a comma, because some people don't have their first name in the database of my autoresponder. If you put "Dear" here, it looks stupid without a name. It's a little thing, but it is part of email etiquette. If you're not in control of your database or your autoresponder software, little things like that can make you look foolish.

The next part is just like a sales letter. You're going to have a subhead, the opening hook to your email—the first paragraph, the first line. Then you're going to have the body copy, which will contain your core message.

I got an email the other day that was one big long block of text. It was about two pages long, about some home business opportunity. A solid block is completely useless. No one's going to read that unless it's from Grandma. Yet you see this kind of mistake—a useless chunk of body copy, with no hook, no call to action, no nothing.

One common problem, particularly among new email marketers, is that what they're sending is inherently boring. It's not interesting to anyone except themselves. Are you really having any dialogue with your subscribers, so that you have any sense of what they're interested in? This is difficult to teach, because in some ways, you either get it or you don't. Do you know how to write from a second-person point of view, which engages the reader?

Next, is there any news? Is there any excitement in what you're saying? A lot of emails are pure delivery of content, but it might as well have been ripped out of a phone book. It's just not interesting. Again, are you excited when you're writing it? Do you think someone else would be excited to read it?

I don't have a formula for not making a boring email. I think the odds are that if everyone's already talked about something, if it's old news or if it's just something you feel you have to deliver because it's there, you probably can skip that email.

In one email I sent, I pointed out that some of my marketing guru friends have had their emails land in my junk folder. This is a hot topic: whether your email is getting delivered and where it's getting delivered. I promised a benefit: if they read this article, they're going to learn how to easily avoid having that happen to them, so that's the body of my email.

The Call to Action

After the body text comes the call to action, which is generally the link you want the recipient to click. It's the equivalent of the order form in a direct mail piece.

Sometimes the email is missing a call to action even when there is a link: you don't really make people do what you want them to do or even encourage them to. You just have the link there and hope that out of the goodness of their heart, they'll check out whatever you have.

From a spiritual or metaphysical level, I often find that this happens because the person is insecure about money. They don't actually want to make the money. Or they feel selling is dark or bad or pushy. Or they don't really believe in what they're selling. Maybe it's a business opportunity or product they haven't actually used themselves, or they don't feel rock-solid about it. Are you excited about the product? That's a pretty good litmus test. If you are, you probably won't run into this problem.

If an email's results are poor, look at the call to action. How strong is it? If it's not strong, you might want to do a sanity check and ask why. Maybe your whole business venture really isn't something you're passionate about. Maybe you're just doing it for the money, but you don't really believe in it.

Then there is a signature piece, where you're going to identify yourself a little: that goes with your name. Here too there is a difference of opinion. Some people believe that emails feel more personal when signed just with your name.

Finally, there's the P.S., which is like a second headline. The P.S. is extremely effective with conventional sales letters, though there is some different of opinion about whether it's equally so in emails.

Sometimes subscribers give you feedback on a usability issue. Pay attention to that, because that's where the rubber hits the road. If they can't read your email, or if it's a pain, you don't have much goodwill. People may not feel like taking the time right now to deal with the issue. They put it off till later, and later always turns into the ever-flowing stream of distraction. They probably won't come back unless they really like you.

Sometimes you may get the same offer from five or six different people. You may wonder what impact this has on its validity. When a big campaign is going out for a product and a lot of affiliates are sending out the same piece of mail, people will tend to buy from the one they have the best relationship with. They'll pick the person they feel most comfortable with and trust. It doesn't matter if they got the email first or last. That is the rarest commodity online: the connection with subscribers. If you don't have a differentiation, if you don't have the human bond, it's just a bunch of junk to be deleted. You've got to stand out as a human being.

People are pragmatic: they will go the distance for value. If you don't provide any value, if you're not adding any content of your own, who needs you?

Audio and Video

Audio postcards in emails can be very effective. Some people have had outrageous response to audio postcards. AudioGenerator (audiogenerator.com) is a proven formula, and it's affordable. Audio helps to build the relationship. It's the magnet to let people know that you're a human being. It brings in a more rounded, human dimension.

Video postcards are the next level, but they involve another level of sophistication. To a certain extent, audio is audio. If we can hear it, if it's comprehensible, it's enough. But poor video quality is distracting. A home video look can affect the perception of quality.

In any event, audio and video bring in people that are otherwise lost in the world of text—dyslexics, for example. They won't sit there with a computer screen and read a twenty-page sales letter.

There is also a gender issue. Women, especially mothers, don't have time to go through lengthy content. They pass by most of the material written by men, because it appeals more to a male audience. They often feel, "I just don't have time."

By the way, I see a lot of emails whose tone is rather apologetic, like, "Sorry to bother you; I know you're busy." Don't do that. You'll come across as believing that you're bothering them and you're trying to compensate somehow. I recommend abandoning that position.

Build a List of Fans

Don't just have subscribers. Build a list of fans. Think of it in terms of creating a relationship where they think you're the most amazing thing ever. Look at Oprah. She is a human being, a woman, and everybody knows who she is. Yet she's also a brand. When she talks about people, they have been instantly cast into the glow. All of a sudden, they are celebrities in their own right. Furthermore, everyone identifies with Oprah's personal story, which has some very dramatic and engaging elements. Include personal stories in your marketing. Tie that to your content.

Some do it another way. They say, "This is my personal story, and this is what's going on with me right now." Then they go into the material. On the whole, it's best to tie the story into the material. If you don't, you're just saying, "All right. This is me being social." That either works for your list or it doesn't.

It depends on how you train your list. If from your first email you say, "OK. This is our hanging-out time, and this is where I'm teaching you what you're here to learn," people that are into that will stick with you. If they're not, they will unsubscribe. In any case, be authentic; be yourself. If you say, "Hey, the kids went sledding today, and one of them knocked a tooth out. Oh, by the way, hypnotic writing is great," it doesn't connect at all, but it may be exactly why they like you.

Relevant stories that you tie into content are different from autobiography. Tens of thousands of people try to publish books every year. Most of them essentially says, "Hey, here's my story!" Who cares? If you don't make them care, there's no reason for caring. Caring is where you connect, where there's mutual ground. If you don't provide that, you're weakening your marketing.

Business consultant Perry Marshall let you sign up for his travel log while he was going to Australia to teach at a seminar. He was going to be in a number of different countries. He sent out emails saying, "Here's a seven-foot snake that I walked across in Australia." You found yourself oddly wanting to know what was happening to him.

This may be connected to the reality TV phenomenon. The further you get away from being a one-dimensional billboard to someone you might meet at a barbecue, the better your marketing is going to be.

People want support with their personal as well as their professional lives. You can take a principle and teach people to implement it in their everyday lives, showing for example, how to teach your teenager the law of attraction.

You could take any piece of information and translate it into personal terms. Especially in Internet marketing, you can get out of your box and say, "You know, I used this idea in my head when I was talking to my wife." All of a sudden, the reader thinks, "You care a lot more about me than just building my business." That's the Oprah effect: communicating to your audience, "I really care about you."

You can take sharing personal material as far as you want. Everyone relates to it. Some copywriters are willing to expose everything, including screwups. They say, "I'm willing to take everything out of the closet and say, 'You know what? I'm no different than you in how I've had to live my life. Yet I found the answers that I believe will help you.'" One headline asked, "How does an expert that teaches the law of attraction get attacked by a Rottweiler?" The key here is to make yourself vulnerable: "I'm an expert, but guess what? I'm messing up at times too."

The late Gary Halbert, an expert in copywriting and direct marketing, called this "image suicide." Take yourself off the pedestal. Leap off it. Smash it on the floor and say, "Look, this is me." That was a big part of his persona. He did it in a much bigger way than I'm describing here.

At one point I did a survey. Half the people responded, "I don't want to hear anything more about your personal life," and the other half said, "I want to hear more about your personal life."

In my newsletter, there's a little segment, usually at the beginning, that talks about personal things. The margins are a little different: you become trained to know that's where Joe's going to talk about himself. If you're interested, you can read it. If not, skip to the meaty stuff. Many people have written to me and said, "Thanks for sharing your concern about your ex when she was in a nearly fatal car accident" or whatever I've shared.

As a rapport builder, I would say to go ahead and share some of your stories. But don't get on a soapbox and write your autobiography when your readers don't care.

With a fan relationship, the suspension of disbelief is intense. You can say anything. You can really push the envelope. You're going to keep a large majority of your fan base once they're loyal to you.

Building this kind of loyalty can also provide value above and beyond what's expected. Here's an example. After one purchase, I got a series of autoresponder messages saying, "Have you looked at this page? Have you checked this out? This is how you can make that work." Every day it sent me to look at the page. It's all drawing back into what you bought. It encourages you to check out different elements of the product. That is beyond merely providing value. Moreover, as an info marketer, you're encouraging the consumption of your product.

Feel Free to Sell

People sometimes ask about the ratio of content to sales pitch. One rule of thumb is that with 60–70 percent content, you'll be in the green zone.

But there's another aspect to the question. You also have the opportunity to do selling in the content. That's what I call hidden selling. Say you tell a story about something fantastic, but the end result is, you might want to run to Amazon and buy it. In some ways, this is a higher level of selling. You are providing content at the same time that you are selling, so everybody's happy.

There are also times to feel good about just direct selling. If you're delivering what people want to buy, there is no harm in saying, "I want you to buy this. This is why you're on my list. If you believe in learning about this subject, this is what you should have now. If you can't afford it, don't have the time, don't care anymore, that's OK too." They will buy it because they genuinely want to, and you're not twisting their arm. You're not being abusive.

The feeling that selling is bad needs to be addressed. No one is going to stand behind manipulation, hype, or deceit, but I don't think those things are equivalent to selling. People are shy about saying, "Click on the link" because they feel selling is bad. I think we have to wipe out that sentiment. It's useless.

On the other hand, a constant barrage of "Buy this, buy this, buy this, or get off my list" is no good either. Although I once sent out an email saying, "Listen, I'm so passionate about this that if you don't buy it, I question whether you need to be on the list or not. You might want to consider unsubscribing."

This is not, incidentally, the same as an email I got from one guy who was trying to get started. He was essentially saying, "If you don't buy something, I'm thinking of quitting this gig, because it's just not working out." This goes back to a point I made earlier: Why should I care? What's in it for me? The positioning is all wrong. I'm positioning myself as the expert, yet I'm completely unsuccessful at what I'm doing.

The Power of Negative Talking

I don't approve of berating or belittling your subscribers. I know why it works when it does work, but, as I've said, I don't want to go with negative selling. It's not for me.

I'm not making value judgments. Feel free to use negative selling if you think it's appropriate. It positions you as the dominant person in the relationship. One guy that I've read for years is frequently condescending to subscribers, yet most of the time, he stays behind a line where it still seems OK.

As for controversy, Howard Stern is a very polarizing person. Yet one statistic suggested that people that dislike him listen to him longer than the ones that like him. Being terrified of offending anybody in your list may not be useful. To the extent that it fits your niche, what you're trying to do, and how you see yourself, if you can generate some sort of controversy or PR, by all means go ahead.

One person who does that is Randy Gage, a very hard-hitting, in-your-face type of prosperity guru. I love him because he blows the whistle on delusional beliefs that we take in and accept. He writes articles that begin: "I'm in Paris, on the water, drinking coffee, and I'm staying at this hotel, and it was built in the 1800s." Then he'll weave in some thoughts about prosperity: where did you choose to go for your vacation, and where did you choose to stay? Then he will lead into his prosperity course: you can buy his audios for a couple hundred bucks, you can buy his five series of books, or you can sign up for his next seminar.

Again, it begins with an interesting personal story. It's unusual. It's in your face. Then he goes into the beliefs and thoughts he's trying to communicate. He asks questions to get you involved. The next thing you know, you're about to sign an order form. I really admire what he's doing. He is sharing himself. The Randy Gage approach is to begin by telling a little bit about yourself and what you're doing. The tie it in a hypnotic way to whatever you're trying to sell.

Mental Word Pictures

David Garfinkel is a master copywriter and a master teacher of copywriting. He uses metaphors and talks about creating mental word pictures. One example: "How an advertising secret that created a six-year backlog in orders for pianos can get you more business than you ever imagined possible."

The six-year backlog is the gotcha here. What does a six-year backlog look like for most businesses? Also, it's for pianos. How does that happen? You're going to click on this link. What kind of backlog can I create for my business?

Internet marketer Armand Morin has tested and found that the more often he puts a link in his email, the more response it has. You can put it in the front, the middle, and the end. I have some concern about this approach, because some of the spam filters or ISPs will say, "Oh, you've got more than a couple of links? You are a spammer." A compromise is to go with two links in the email, then test to see if it goes through. Everything that you're doing with your email copy has to factor in filters.

Then there are soap opera emails. With this approach, you generate curiosity in the subject line. You're saying, "I'm withholding information now with the intent of getting you to do something." But you have to deliver. Failing to come through is a bad thing to do.

One great approach: use the initial curiosity to get the reader into the body of the email. Satisfy that initial curiosity, if at all possible, in that email. Then open up a new thing to be curious about. This will get them to want to do the next thing—to click on the link. It's a chain of curiosity.

Pay attention to this principle throughout your email copy. Ask, does this paragraph follow any sort of curiosity chain? Is it broken anywhere? Does the copy answer every question? Then who cares about going to the link?

This is also a way of subconsciously building credibility with the reader. You've generated curiosity in the subject line and satisfied it. You've built a bond by delivering. Then, being a marketer, you're going to open up something new to be curious about. They're more likely to trust you to provide that too. Once you've done that two or three times, you'll have established a pattern that will stand in your favor.

The Zeigarnik Effect

Copywriter Frank Garon will send out an email that's a shocker. One had the subject line, "What I learned getting clocked by my boss." His boss actually decked him at the car shop that he worked at. The whole purpose of this email is to get attention, so the next time you get an email from him, you're more likely to open it. It's a door opener. The second or third email is where the cash register rings.

Frank turned that incident into an attention-getter. What did he learn from that? Why did he attribute something good to it? On the surface, it doesn't make sense that that would be good, so you have to read the copy. Then he hinted that there was another announcement coming later. He got everybody stirred up. The next email had to do with mentoring and brought in several thousand dollars.

In this example, Frank used two emails. You can also work with sets of three, where people receive a series of three emails on the subject. A series of threes is a good pattern.

Frank sticks with this approach. Periodically, he'll lob an emotional pop and get people stirred up. It's controversy. It's attention. It's change. It's difference. It has to do with pattern recognition. We notice differences. We don't notice when something is the same.

This is called the *Zeigarnik effect*, after Soviet psychologist Bluma Zeigarnik. Mark Joyner popularized it in his book *MindControlMarketing.com: How Everyday People Are Using Forbidden Mind Control Psychology and Ruthless Military Tactics to Make Millions.* (I wrote the foreword.)

The Zeigarnik effect has to do with the fact that the mind has an urge to monitor patterns. It's essentially a pattern recognition system. When a pattern is not completed or there's something missing, the mind desires to fix that and get it solved.

In terms of the brain, Broca's area, the motor speech area, listens to all of the information coming into the brain. Broca's area is located inside your brain, directly behind your ears. It has the purpose of listening to information. It's looking for the predictable, the mundane, the already known. If you had to pay attention to every single thing that's required for you to function, there's no way you could do it. You could not have your attention spread in that many directions at one time.

Broca's area is constantly listening for the mundane in order to move it through and say, "I don't need to pay attention to this." When you surprise Broca's area, you get people's attention. When your writing affects people, or they have to answer a question they don't know the answer to, you surprise Broca's area.

Wernicke's area focuses on verbs, on action, and on words related to that. Hypnotic writing influences you to go right past Broca's area into Wernicke's area and start taking action.

Your Inbox University

By the way, your own inbox is university on how to write good copy. If it works on you, if you like it, then it's probably an option for you. Here's one possibility: "I got to tell you about this!" English teachers don't like it. At the same time, doesn't it convey excitement? Isn't it something you would say if you saw a good movie, ate in a good restaurant, or read a great book? It's a brilliant intro for a newsletter.

Another way in which your inbox is your university is to see how people are selling you. Even if I don't always buy the product, I'll at least learn from it.

Mailing Logistics

Let's go on to more technical matters, starting with the opt-in. This is where some flat tires can occur in your process. Make sure to ask your subscriber to whitelist you when they're opting in. You may not get another shot, because your follow-up email can be deleted by their filter.

Whitelist is the opposite of blacklist. With the blacklist, you're blocked. You can't get in. You're in the doghouse. Whitelist, on the other hand, means anything you send comes in without question. If you want to subscribe to something, you say, "I at least want to give this a couple of issues to check it out. I'll whitelist it for now." You can always ditch it later.

You should have a step that says, "Will you confirm?" A lot of people won't: "No, I won't. I'm sorry; I don't have the time to sit there and confirm." Still, you should give them the chance.

Anyway, tell them what to do. Tell them to whitelist you when they're opting in. It's part of your process. It's particularly important in the double opt-in process. *Double opt-in* means that they've requested it, and you've made them confirm their request, either on a web page or in an email. Let's say your email is going to say, "Your MrFire subscription requires confirmation." Tell them that that's what the subject is going to say, and it's happening right now. It's not going to come in a couple of days. You don't have to say, "Hey, it's an autoresponder," but let them know that this action is there to take in the next couple of seconds, not hours. You don't want them to put the message in the "later" box, because that will kill your conversion rate.

Mail to your list at least once a week, just to stay in front of them. That's a minimum, although it will vary with your niche and your situation. You can even send out mailings three or four times a week without being flamed. The more you can be in front of your readers, the more mind share you can have, at least for those who are opening the emails. Those who never open your email— we don't care about them anyway. If they're not interested enough, don't even worry about it. They're not likely to be effective subscribers.

If you're planning out an e-course, warm up the list first. Some marketers will even send seven to ten emails of pure content before even broaching the subject of selling. You're making the human element of reciprocity kick in here. You're giving first. The recipient thinks, "Wow!

OK. If I'm called upon, I will give back in the form of"—whatever, an opt-in, or "go here," "check this out," "come to this teleseminar." This is the footwork of building a bond.

Target who your email is for. This is not just a matter of "Hey, are you in a target market?" When you're in your autoresponder and you have a bunch of different sub lists, make sure that you select the right one. If you have a copywriting offer, make sure that it goes to your sub list on copywriting. Target, because everything else you do after this will depend on who you're sending it to. You don't tell your grandmother about your wild night out.

Reason out why you are writing. This is where you're going to create the excitement that generates the subject line. Why are you sending this? What's the urgency? What's the core of the offer? Know what this is. Once you identify it, you'll be able to polish it and make it stronger.

Again, make sure you're writing to one person. Don't say, "Hey, lots of you have said . . ." If that subscriber hasn't said it, don't tell them that. That person didn't complain or give feedback. Instead, you can say, "Hey, lots of the other subscribers . . ."

Another tip for dealing with filters: get yourself an account on Outlook, Gmail, Yahoo!, Hotmail, and the rest and put yourself on your list. Mail to yourself. Did you go in the junk folder? Did it merge code correctly? Did it have fifty characters? Did one of them shoot across the screen?

Next: no boring emails. Here the test is, would you read this email if it weren't in your self-interest? Step out of yourself. Have a dialogue, as I recommended earlier. Would you care about this?

As I've already said, let other people read your copy first, especially if it's an important promotion. Have some knowledgeable peers and even some newbies read it and give you feedback. Do you have an authentic voice? Or do you just sound like everybody else?

Check: is there a call to action? Did you forget the link? Do your links work? Do you have a P.S.? Do you want to use one? That's worth thinking about. Have you included your signature, your name, who you are, your branding? By law, you also need to provide an unsubscribe process that's clear and functional.

5

Influence versus Manipulation

There's a psychological phenomenon called *inattentional blindness*. Say you've gotten in a car and started driving down the road to go across town. Fifteen minutes later, you're across town, and as you're parking your car, you realize, "Wow! I have no idea how I got here. I don't remember which route I took. I don't remember what happened along the way, but now I'm here." That is inattentional blindness. You were inattentionally blind to everything that was happening around you. Inattentional blindness is one of the biggest causes of accidents in industrial environments. People get so used to repetitive motion that they don't pay attention to what they're doing. They're inattentionally blind to it.

The same thing happens when you write placid copy. It doesn't pull people in. It doesn't get them to start an internal dialogue so that they're able to express themselves: "Yes, I can see myself taking this action." That's how you can see ten commercials in a row without remembering any of them. They try to sell everything the same way to the same people, and nobody's sales increases.

The Earworm Effect

There are times when you hear a song, and it's stuck in your mind for the rest of the day. Today this is sometimes called an *earworm*. It's a phonological loop. You want people to create these phonological loops about you. When people think about hypnotic writing, the next thing that should come to mind is Joe Vitale. "Joe Vitale—yeah, the hypnotic writing guy."

This creates a challenge. If, say, I wanted to become the ice climbing king, that's a big, incongruent switch, so I have to create a new loop. But good writing can do that.

This phenomenon happens with character actors. People can't imagine them any other way. John Travolta is a perfect example. He started out in films like *Saturday Night Fever* and *Grease*. Then he was nothing. Nobody could imagine him in any other roles. Then he was reinvented with *Pulp Fiction*, where he played a gangster.

After that, you didn't have any problems seeing John Travolta as a tough bad guy. Now if he were to go back to his role in *Saturday Night Fever,* that would be a big shift for a lot of people who didn't already know him that way.

This psychology has to do with branding. Branding is nothing more than accumulations of thoughts, feeling, ideas, and actions that you've taken around a certain thought. Brand only exists in your customer's mind. It doesn't exist anywhere else. Brand doesn't exist in a logo, in a business card, in a website. Brand only exists in people's minds. Whatever perception you create for them about you is what they're going to remember about you. That's your brand.

That's why so many people go through rebranding exercises, but nothing happens. That's because the public has already created a very powerful association with what they believe the brand is. Changing a logo does not change your brand. But changing the voice that you give your company may change your brand. Again, it takes time because you have to realign people's ideas of who and what you are.

The Fine Line

There is a very fine line between manipulation and influence. Manipulation is always negative. It's designed to break people down to their lowest form and get them to take some action that you want them to take for your own benefit and no one else's.

Influence is always positive. It's powerfully moving for people in a way that's helpful and beneficial. You have the greater good of someone else in mind. You're helping them move forward to a better position than they are in today. Manipulation is helping *me* move forward, using *you*, to the place that *I* want to be today. Manipulation is all about me using you. Influence is all about me assisting you.

Influence gets us a giant wad of cash gift wrapped and handed to us on a silver platter. People are happy to give gifts. It's exciting. It makes us feel good, right? I'm giving you something of value. You're going to say, "Yes, I'll take it." Why? Because at some level, you've influenced me enough to make me believe that you're a worthy person, somebody I'd want to give something to.

Manipulation gets us some things too. It can get you anything you want in life in the very short term, but ultimately it gets you a ride to prison. Manipulators are often known as hustlers, con men, shysters, cheats, home-wreckers, heartbreakers, and eventually almost always as criminals. Practically all manipulators end up getting caught, because they self-destruct. You can only do this for so long. You can only be out of congruence with yourself for so long before you ultimately give it up.

The Power of Cults

The most difficult beliefs to change are those that are pro-grammed from early birth. Some people are brought up in very strict religious cults, which teach that if you've ever been divorced, you're going to hell. If you're a woman who wears pants or has cut your hair, you're going straight to hell. If you're a man who has ever had lustful thoughts about a woman—straight to hell.

You might think, "That's ridiculous. What in the world would make you think that way?" When you're a child, you don't have those choices. At seven years old, you can't make the choice to pack up your bags and live with some-body else. That just doesn't exist. Control is a big key here.

Here's an example of a cult: the Army. You either get along in the Army and you do very well, or you don't do very well at all. It's designed to get you to do certain kinds of things. The Army takes genuinely good people. Within a period of about thirteen weeks, it turns them into peo-ple who are more than willing to go at the drop of a hat and kill other human beings. Is that cultish behavior? Yes. Is it appropriate behavior? It's arguable. But it's appropri-ate behavior for our societal standards today.

Another example of a cult is the Drug Enforcement Administration. A DEA agent is very effective at getting people to sell him illicit drugs. Why? Because it's easy to influence people to do something that they're already naturally inclined to do.

A DEA agent doesn't go up to somebody and say, "Let me show you how to go out and get drugs. Then I want you to get them, bring them back here, and then sell them to me. See, that would be really cool. Then you go to prison." No agent would do that.

A good DEA agent gets so adept at doing these things and modeling people who sell drugs at a very high level that he can walk into a bar or hotel, and within ten minutes, he can tell who is selling drugs. Within fifteen minutes, this person will be selling to him. You do this by building a persona, based on the principles of influence. If you understand this, you have the keys to unethically open up the pocketbook of any person you meet from now on.

To explore the difference between influence and manipulation, there are some valuable lessons to be learned from cults, particularly about presenting information and moving large groups. The power of a cult lies in those abilities.

I'm going to present some information that will give you everything that you need to know to unethically but powerfully manipulate people. If you're at all inclined to do that, if you find that at all amusing or intriguing, then I'd like you to please be honest with yourself and skip this material, because it will be devastating. It would be doing you an incredible disservice.

Manipulators make use of the following emotional appeals to get their way:

Guilt. Guilt is the number one thing. In a cult, how do they use guilt? If you leave the church, you can never come back. You can never see your family, and they are going to watch you burn in hell. That's a very big amount of guilt, particularly when you're young and inexperienced.

Intimidation. Cults have strongmen who can beat you up. There's real joy in that if you're a manipulator.

Ego attack. "You're no good. You're worthless. God doesn't love you unless you're following us. Your husband, your wife, your family won't love you." If I break your ego down enough, I can manipulate you. Eventually I can get you to believe anything.

If you don't believe me, go to any battered women's shelter. These are people whose egos have been detached from them, broken down, crushed. They have to rebuild from some base level before they can restore themselves.

Fear. Fear is an unbelievable motivator if you're a manipulator. If you're in a church, it's fear of going to hell. You're going to burn forever, and your family isn't going to be with you. You'll be separated from them for eternity.

Fear of this kind can be very powerful. Elizabeth Smart is a good example. She was a little girl who was kidnapped by a religious fanatic in Salt Lake City in 2002. He told her, "If you leave this house, even though you're completely unchained and nothing can stop you, we will kill your family. You'll regret it for the rest of your life."

Love. The inappropriate use of love: "We love you, and we care about you, and other people don't. If you want to be part of our family and you really love me, you'll do this for me." Again, it's all about me.

Being liked. We all want to be liked by someone. We all want to be liked by a group. Here's how to manipulate someone with an email list: "I'm just going to cut you out of my list. You won't be part of the group anymore."

"No, no, wait; I want to be part of the group."

"No, you can't; sorry. If you want to be part of the group, you need to go out and get fifty-two new people to sign up with you. When you do, you'll have proven your worthiness to me, and I'll let you back in."

Lies. Manipulators can lie. To manipulators it's OK to lie. There's no value in *not* lying, because everything else you've done is about destroying somebody's capacity for making good decisions. The lie is probably the least of the steps. You've already done so many other things that at this point, it just doesn't matter. It doesn't matter that there's no truth when I said, "God came and talked to me individually, and he told me to tell you that you're going to hell."

If I told you that I had a quick prayer session with God today, and God told me that you are going to hell, you'd say, "Go to hell yourself! You're ridiculous." It's just not going to happen. But if I crushed you and destroyed your ego, you would probably agree. You'd say, "Yeah, I do need to be different. I do need to act differently. I need to go with the flow."

Marketers intentionally or unintentionally manipulate people instead of influencing them. It's OK if we just lie a little, because what we do call lies in marketing? Spin, right? "Just spin it a little bit differently." They can justify these deceits.

That's what manipulation is all about. Manipulation is all about *me*. It's about getting whatever I desire, no matter what the cost. Many victims of manipulation never recover. They carry the scars for the rest of their life. Look at *20/20*, look at *60 Minutes*, or any of the news shows. You'll see example after example of people who are smart, logical, realistic, yet were manipulated in horrible ways. That's exactly how not to be.

If you're a manipulator, you should build your story in chunks. If I came into a church and talked about how cults influence people, and I did it in such a way that their beliefs and their dogma fell right in line with what I was saying about cults, would I be manipulating people into thinking differently about their church? Or would I just be drawing a line between myself and them? They'd say, "He's trying to say our church is a cult, and we don't believe that."

If you push manipulation too far, at some point people say, "Hey, look, I don't believe it. It's nonsense." You have to elicit just enough information so that you can feed it back. You lay the story out in chunks as appropriate. The story that's true for you won't be the same story that's true for another person.

By moving incrementally, you can manipulate people to the point where they're willing to harm themselves. If I come up to you and I try to manipulate you by throwing everything at you at once, it won't work. It would be like splashing you in the face with hot water. You'd scream and run away. You build the desire slowly over time.

I'm not telling you specifically how to go about that kind of manipulation. If you want to figure that out how, all you need to do is watch Sunday morning preachers on television, or old videos of carnival barkers and people like that. You'll see how they do it. It's very specific and methodical.

At the end of the day, does a carnival barker have your best interests or his best interests in mind? Does a Sunday morning preacher have your best interests in mind or his? They would like you to believe that they have your best interests in mind, but what is their real goal? They want you to give them money. They aren't ethical enough to say, "Listen, don't take your last $10, put it in an envelope, and mail it to me. Do not do that. That's the worst possible thing you could do for yourself." But they know that people will cash in a $5 food stamp for $2.50, put the $2.50 in an envelope, and mail it off to the preacher. They prey on those people.

Don't be predatory. Never manipulate, but always influence. Influence gets you what you want in life, and it gets everyone else what they want in life.

How to Influence People

Let's talk about the characteristics of influence. These are a lot lighter.

Transference. Transference is taking my reputation, my power, people's belief in me and transferring it to you. If you trust me and I recommend someone else, you immediately listen. You don't evaluate. Transference is one of the key principles to influence: linking one to another.

How do you use transference in your writing? With testimonials. Testimonials imply transference of power. It's linking me to you: "This person, whom I already trust and respect, says it's OK." I can logically assume that they're not telling me a lie, because they never have in the past.

The desire to believe. A lot of people have a desire to believe certain things. You particularly see this in religious movements. People have a desire to believe something, so they're very susceptible to the message. In marketing, when we're selling things, we're creating that desire to believe. How? By selling to people who are very targeted and who have identified themselves with those who want to get this kind of information. They've indicated that they have a desire to believe, for example, that email marketing is valuable. They have a desire to believe that they can get people to open up their pockets by sending a letter to them or driving them to a website. The desire to believe targets those people who most desire to believe.

Social proof. If everyone else is doing it, I should probably do it too, right? It's like the lemmings: we all run off the edge of the cliff together.

Social proof is demonstrating that people are already on board and giving others the confidence to take the same action. If you see 10,000 people walking down the street towards flames, it's a whole lot easier to do yourself. If they're all doing it, it must be safe.

Social proof manifests in other ways. If five people start looking up at something, even if nothing is there, others will look up too. They won't see anything, but they'll assume they're not seeing what everyone else is. Social proof is telling me that there must be something I should look at, because all these people wouldn't be standing there staring at nothing. One study done in New York City showed that people actually did this.

That's why email marketing can be tremendously effective. It's social proof, especially when you get it from somebody you trust.

At some level, though, too much social proof causes people to question whether something is valid or not. "Everybody's doing it. I don't want to be one of the pack. I want to be different." Everybody wants to be part of a pack, but at some level, the pack gets too big for everybody, and they want to drop out.

Consistency. Delivering the message in a manner that's consistent with expectations. People have certain expectations about how they want to receive information. The value comes from understanding how to deliver it. There's a consistent format that was designed by someone at some point and accepted by others. I need to follow that format. Then I'll be delivering it in such a way that people will want to accept the information from me.

Storytelling. This is an important element of influence. It's what undercover police officers use to survive. If you're an undercover officer, a lot of times, you're going in with no gun, no badge, and no backup. Backup is a block down the street, sitting in a van. But people can do all kinds of things to you in the time it takes to move a block. You have to have an impeccable story that compels people to believe you.

Here's an example from real life. A guy who had been buying drugs from an undercover cop walked up to him. He had a long trench coat, pulled a shotgun out, and put it to his head. He showed the cop a picture of himself in uniform and said, " I know you're a cop."

"You're nuts. Just put the gun down. This is ridiculous."

"Look at this picture."

"Oh, yeah, the picture? What can I say? Wow, that's uncanny. That's bizarre. That guy does look like me."

It was a matter of getting in rapport with the drug dealer very quickly, of influencing him with every fiber of one's being. It was absolutely certain that the dealer would pull the trigger. He had already sold the cop fifteen pounds of heroin. He would be going to prison for a very long time.

This conversation dragged out for over forty minutes. At the end, the dealer put the gun down and said, "You're right. That is uncanny."

Having a story that is impenetrable, that you can fall back on without even thinking, is so important. Yet most business owners don't know how to create a story about themselves.

Why do people want to listen to stories? We're programmed from a very young age to listen to them. We automatically look for the point to the story. It tells us how to live or what to do or what action to take next. Stories are palatable because they involve our emotions. They get us to think. They get us to move forward. By telling a story, you enthrall people much more easily.

A story is filled with action words, with verbs, with metaphor. The secret key to writing great copy that gets people to move is verbs. Verbs get people to take action. Writing in the third person does nothing. Nobody wants to hear your third-person, objective viewpoint. If you want me to take action, get me involved in the process. Put me into the action. The verbs in your story are what will get me to move.

Change your website from just giving information to telling a story. Mold it into a story of what's happened and how it's going to affect your audience, and get them to move forward. When you do that, you greatly increase the likelihood that they're going to act. You're also reinforcing your brand, because a brand is easier to accept through a story. People will make their own associations based on the story you tell, because they understand that this is the fastest and easiest way to get information.

Authority. Expert status in any form—author, PhD, speaker, celebrity—all position the influencer as somebody who should be believed and trusted. If you're not a recognized expert in your industry, you need to build your expertise. Suppose I call you and say, "Hey, you don't know me from anybody, but I want to call you and talk to you. I like your stuff. I think we should do something together sometime." You're going to say, "You and fifty other guys have called me in the last week."

But if I call you up and say, "Hey, I'm the author of *Making Marketing Work*. I have a radio program called *Making Marketing Work*, and I want to talk to you a little." Does that give me a whole different level of access to Joe now? Absolutely. Does it give me a different level of access to other people around Joe? Absolutely. Creating that expertise also makes you more believable and more able to influence people. You don't question people who are experts, do you? You don't even question people who are perceived experts. That's an important thing to know.

A famous study at Yale was carried out by psychologist Stanley Milgram. It's called the Milgram experiment. The researchers invited subjects in. They had volunteers in white coats, with clipboards in their hands. On each clipboard was a piece of paper with a checklist. The subject sat behind a one-way mirror. Outside, a third person was sitting in front of a board that was attached to electrodes. This person had to memorize a list of words. If they didn't get the list right, the subject had to give them a shock. If the other person didn't get it right the next time, the subject was supposed to increase the shock. This went on up to the point where the shock could be potentially deadly.

The person with the clipboard would say, "OK. Go ahead." The subject would read off the list of words. The person outside the glass would miss the guess. The subject would crank up the electricity so that the person outside would get a still bigger shock. It would get to the point where the people on the other side of the window were saying, "Please don't shock me anymore. I can't take it anymore. Don't do it."

But the clipboard person would say, "Increase the voltage; do it again," and 65 percent of the people would increase the voltage to the point of being potentially deadly.

The only person who was not an actor in the situation was the subject, the person they invited in to deliver the shock. Everybody else knew exactly what was going on. There was no real shock delivered. The person outside the glass was an actor hired to pretend to be shocked.

But the subjects believed they were delivering real, and painful, shocks. They obeyed because the people who were directing them were in a position of authority. They had white lab coats, they had clipboards. So, the subjects reasoned, these were the ones they should listen to, even though they believed their actions were causing severe pain and possibly death: "They know better than I do about what's going on, so I'll listen to them."

When somebody perceived as an authority says something, we are likely to accept it as true, whether that person is a policeman, a minister, or a high-school teacher. The more you establish yourself as an authority, the more likely you are to be successful in selling.

Familiarity. The more familiar you are with someone, the more likely you are to act on their recommendation. Before you buy anything, you have to trust the person who's selling.

So first, develop the familiarity. You may have to send five to seven emails to someone before trying to sell them anything. You get them to know who you are and what you're about. You show your essence: "This is who I am; this is what I'm about. I'm a giving, caring person. I'm giving you this information at no charge so you can get to know who I am before I ask for anything."

Scarcity. How valuable are my printed books? It depends on whom you ask, but if I put some of those that are out of print on eBay, somebody would go out and pay a tremendous amount of money for them, because they're scarce.

If the book is out of print, and it's not available anywhere else, it's worth a lot more money. The scarcer, the more unavailable you can make something, the more likely it is to influence someone to take action. If you're in the know, if you're in the inner circle, if you have access to information that not everyone can get, it's a very scarce commodity.

This is why people can charge tens of thousands of dollars for seminars. Motivational speaker Tony Robbins charges amounts like that for some of his programs. He openly says that only a certain number of people can ever reach this portal to pure nirvana. It's very scarce, and you want that, don't you? Everybody does. Everybody wants to get there.

There is a flip side to that, however. The sitcom *Frasier* had a spa episode. Frasier and his brother, Niles, go to a spa in Seattle and see a gold door. What's behind the gold door? They're told, "Oh, if you haven't been invited, you can't go behind the gold door. It's only for special people."

This drives Frasier crazy. He can't take it. He's got to get behind the golden door. He has his assistant call in a favor from a senator. The senator says, "Oh, yeah. They have the most exotic treatments you'll ever find back there. Maidens will slather you with honey butter."

Frasier gets the recommendation. The next time and Niles go back behind the golden door, they're having a great old time. It's wonderful. It's pure bliss. Then they notice that there's a platinum door. Frasier says, "We've got to get behind the platinum door." He asks one of the staff, who replies, "No, sir, you're not allowed back there. Only certain people can go behind the platinum door."

This too drives him crazy. He and Niles go over and realize that the platinum door is unlocked. They've got masks on and cucumber slices over their eyes. They open the door and they say, "Oh my God! It's beautiful. Light. It's so warm. I can feel the heat penetrating every ray of my body. It's heaven."

The door shuts. Frasier and Niles turn around and find it's locked. They say, "What's that smell? It's an aroma of—" and they take their cucumbers off their eyes. There are dumpsters right in front of them. They've walked out of the platinum door into the dumpster alley.

When you're selling exclusive things, at some point the nirvana runs out.

Exclusivity. This is a similar concept. If only a limited number of people have access to something and it's exclusive, it must be valuable. By admitting someone to this group, you give a person whom you desire to influence something that other people can't have. That enables you to influence them even more.

Say I tell you, "Listen, there's a lot more to this program that I'm not going to teach you here. In fact, I teach the same program to law enforcement and to the CIA. I show them how to influence people in thirty seconds or less. Only a limited number of people can take advantage of it. I'm very selective about the people I teach it to, because some of them are not honest. I'll be able to tell whether you are by talking to you. Call me. We'll spend thirty minutes on the phone together. I'll be able to determine whether or not you're the ethical, honest person you say you are. If you are, I'll consider you for the training. If you're not, then I'm going to call you out. It'll never be available to you. I'll expressly forbid anybody who ever learns from me to teach you."

If someone says that to you, wouldn't you think, "I'd kind of like to know what that's about"? That's what exclusivity does.

You can use exclusivity in a fear-based form: "You will never get this information if you don't act today. If you don't, there will be no way you can ever get to it." That's a fear-based model, as opposed to saying, "There are steps that you have to take in this process, and you may not be able to do it now, but you could in the future."

It's all about the customer again, encouraging them to take action that they're already inclined to take. They've proven that they're inclined to take it, because you're advertising to people who have already shown a willingness to accept information from you. These people are not being inappropriately manipulated. They're being influenced to take some action. You're simply encouraging them to take the step more quickly.

Curiosity. This is one of my favorite techniques. I used it when I spoke to the National Guild of Hypnotists, the largest hypnosis convention in the world: 2,000 hypnotists fly in from all over the world. They asked me to speak on hypnotic writing. I began by saying, "I can say three words, and you'll give me all your money. I can say eight words, and you'll never have money worries again. Are you curious?"

I began with that. I made sure the audience wants to know the answer. Are you curious? Do you want to know the answer? Great. I move on, because it opens a door in their mind. They are waiting. I don't satisfy their curiosity for a long time.

You can use this yourself. This is a million-dollar technique. If you can build on curiosity and keep building it to a crescendo, you'll have a tremendous amount of influence. Some people would whip out their checkbooks and write a huge check to me just to know what those eleven words are.

Empathy. Sharing feelings or common issues encourages people to get on our side.

Reciprocation. This works by simply giving someone something first. If you give something away, you get something back. Now this is a dirty little secret, but your parents did this to you at a very early age. "Your sister just gave you a hug; hug her back. If she gives you a hug, you have to give her a hug." "Those people gave you candy. Now you be nice and go give them a muffin." It's built into us from a very young age. If I give you something, you have to give me something back.

You've heard of the law of reciprocation. Every one of us is affected by it at some level. When someone does something for us, we feel obligated to do something in return. It's a strong social dictate. If you're consciously aware of this process, you can decide not to go along with it. But if I'm persistent enough in giving you something, at some point the power of reciprocation will kick in. You're going to take some action.

Think about it. What can you give people? It doesn't have to be anything of tremendous value. That's why the federal government will no longer let employees go to lunch with someone who pays for it. The impulse to give something in return is so high that it can result in a huge loss of money. A $60 lunch ends up costing the government millions of dollars, because a contract has been awarded to someone who was woefully unqualified or charged too much. Reciprocation is that powerful.

Inconsequence. By taking an action that seems inconsequential or small, people are more likely to take another action. If an undercover cop is buying drugs, he wouldn't walk up to somebody and go, "Hey, buddy. How about selling me a kilo of crack?"

The first thing the cop would do is get the suspect to play a game of pool with him for five bucks. It's illegal. You're not supposed to gamble in most states. But it's inconsequential, because everybody plays for money. Then the agent might start talking about partying and how many times he's been high and drunk and messed up, and about all his buddies who are doing the same thing. Pretty soon he has the suspect in the palm of his hand. He has tremendous influence over this guy just by starting with a simple, inconsequential $5 pool game.

Persona. Your persona enables you to set yourself apart from everyone else. You can set yourself apart by the clothes you wear, by the things you do, by your mannerisms, or by your speech patterns. Any of those things can be combined to set yourself apart.

One way of setting yourself apart is the way you dress. People dress more and more informally these days, but say someone comes into a presentation wearing a suit and tie. Do you suddenly pay more attention? Do you think, "I need to listen to that"? The speaker has set himself apart as an expert, so what he says is less likely to be challenged. You accept it without even thinking, because of his persona, because he set it as a fact: this is the way it is. He has set himself apart.

If you want to be like the people you're with, dress like them. If you want to set yourself apart, do it by your dress, your mannerisms, and the things you do.

There's persona in writing as well. The words you use are the clothes that dress your persona in writing. The better words you use and the more effectively you use them, the more you set yourself apart. You start to see that happen when people pay attention to you versus someone else. They unsubscribe from other people's lists, but they stay on yours. Clothe the persona you create in your writing.

Likability. People are much more apt to take an action suggested by someone they like. Fifty percent of the people in this world may not like me. I'm perfectly OK with that, because the other 50 percent are going to like me.

More than half of the people who read your website will never sign up for an email from you. They don't want anything else from you. They could care less. They don't like you. So what? Who cares? Yet many people want to be liked so much that if you let them in, they'll do what you want. Because guess what? They want to be liked by you.

Relevance. This is the biggest mistake people make in marketing today. I don't care if you're an Internet marketer or if you're selling hot dogs on the street. If you're not relevant to the concerns of the person you're selling to, you can never influence them. If somebody asks me to give to a charity that supports the Ku Klux Klan, that's in no way relevant to me. Would I support them in any possible scenario?

That's a bizarre example, but how many times do people send offers for things that are completely irrelevant to you, like the cream for women that's equal to Viagra? How many of those emails do I get? I'm not, in the furthest stretch of my imagination, going to go out and buy that cream for myself.

If you're going to influence people, only give them information that's relevant to them. Once you've created a bond with them and they've come to expect something from you, don't switch horses in the middle of the stream. Don't throw in something like, "Oh, and by the way, buy this brand-new hairbrush, because it's great and I like it." People don't buy that. It just makes them question your credibility. You've gone through a lot of steps to develop this level of influence. Don't ruin it. Only make offers that are relevant to the audience you're selling to.

Outcome basis. The principles of human influence are outcome-based. The goal is clearly defined ahead of time.

I have a goal of getting you to do something. The goal is appropriate because it's ethical and meaningful. I am going to help you to be a better person as a result. It's presented in a way that allows the person who is being influenced to make the best only and obvious decision.

Notice I haven't said anything about closing people or twisting their arm. I haven't said anything about getting them to take action. All I said was that I've educated them to the point where the only obvious decision they can make is to do what I'm suggesting.

Best-interest focus. The best interest of the person or the group is paramount. It should always be considered as part of the influence process. You have to keep their best interests at heart.

Otherwise people will say at some point, "This is BS. I'm not doing it anymore."

Only a small percentage of people can be manipulated for a long period of time. There's a lot more money in people who want your relevant information and whom you can help grow, as opposed to people that you can control until they don't have anything else to give you.

Truth. Influencers are always truthful. Never lie. There's no good reason to lie to anyone. I didn't say you can't spin your story or put it in the best light, but lies undermine everything you've ever done to influence somebody.

I don't care if the lie is small or large. If you get caught, the person that you've been influencing will immediately question whether anything you've ever told them is true. Think about that in terms of your own experience. What happened when you found out somebody didn't tell you the truth?

In marketing, we've given a lot more leeway. If I say, "You can only get this till August 31," you know that if you call on August 29 of the following year, you can still buy the product. Is that a lie? Technically, yes, it's a lie.

We marketers are given societal latitude. People say, "We know that's a marketing ploy," and they read right past it. But the best people don't use this practice. If they say the offer is through on August 31, that's it. Later they might say, "After much consideration and many requests, I'm releasing this again." But only do it up to a certain point. Then stop and don't do it again. I don't care if people call up and offer you a million dollars for it. You don't sell it again. What do you do if they offer you a million dollars? You sell them the rights to your material. Then they can do whatever they want with it.

Goal and time orientation. Influence is always goal- and time-oriented. You have an outcome in mind. You have a specific time frame in which it has to happen. You don't influence people randomly. You don't influence people forever. You influence them with a particular goal in mind. You're trying to get them to a given point where they take action. Then you start over with your next goal in mind.

Personal orientation. Influencers don't simply pick targets of opportunity. They get to know the people they intend to influence. Carnival barkers pick targets of opportunities, because they know if they throw enough words into an audience, some percentage of the people will come to them. Those people will be unhappy the day after, but it's too late, because what does a carnival inevitably do? Packs up and moves out of town.

A lot of people who do business on the Internet do the same thing. They sell things to people and shut down their website. They're gone never to be seen again. That only accomplishes one thing. It's preparing an audience not to believe what you have to say. It's also creating a much tougher job for everyone else.

Ethics. Influencers focus on ethically moving people in a positive direction, for the best good of those involved. If you start out with a $29 product and ultimately move your customers into a $5,000 product, but you don't believe every step along the way that you're giving them something that's incrementally more valuable, don't sell the product. Stop selling it. Create another product that you can feel good about selling. Otherwise you become a manipulator. Or you end up saying, "I can't even do this anymore. I'd rather flip burgers at McDonald's," because it's not congruent with your own value system. Make sure that your offer is ethical.

6

The Persuasion Equation

Let's talk about how to turn this material into a persuasive tactic that you can use on a regular basis. Position plus presentation times influence equals persuasion.*

Again, we come back to persona. Before beginning the process of persuasion, be sure that you've properly developed your persona. Check your story, clothing, expert status, and presentation. Before you write a single word of copy, make sure you have the credibility to back it up, because people are going to look at that.

---

* I am indebted to Dave Lakhani for much of the material in this chapter.

The Steps to Persuasion

Choose your audience to match your ability. Far too often the persuasion process goes wrong because influencers choose the wrong audience. If you speak to an audience that's used to discussing the neuropsychology of influence, but you come and tell them that you know how to influence people by using five or ten different points, do you think they're going to listen to you? Chances are very high that they won't. They're going to say, "Prove it. Show me conclusive scientific proof that this works." That audience wants to see one particular thing. Selling something that's incongruent with their interests doesn't work.

Spin your story. Build your story in chunks that you can tell to the appropriate audiences. Let's say you want to teach hypnotic writing to a group of massage therapists, a group of New Age clients, and a group of people who are small business retail owners. Even though hypnotic copywriting would be appropriate for all three, would you tell the same story? No, you'll pick out material that's more appropriate for each one. You'll lay in the testimonials that are appropriate to them. You spin your story.

Polish your presentation. Your presentation consists of your story and your persona. As I've said, your persona and writing are the clothes that your words are wrapped in.

Remember the primacy effect: people are more likely to remember the beginning of a list of things. Also remember the recency effect. They remember the thing they heard most recently. If you give people a list, they're going to remember the first two or three things on it. If I list the seven ingredients to success to you, chances are high that you will remember one through three. On the other hand, you may remember four through seven. You tend to remember the first thing you heard or the last thing you heard.

Check your story pieces. Be sure they fit the group you're delivering to. Add any information that needs to be in the story, and make it complete and powerful. Go back and look: Does this story suit this audience? Have I told the whole story? Does it have a beginning, a middle, an end? Does it have influence factors built into it? Have I created emotion? Emotion is what people buy.

Identify objections and possible sticking points in advance. You have my explicit permission to imagine how you think people will respond. Hallucinate if you have to.

Check your wardrobe. Be sure it matches your audience. Check your words to be sure they match your audience and set you apart in a way that elevates your status.

Present powerfully. Use the power of contrast to your benefit. Ask for more than you want first. Then offer what you do want. Say I asked you to buy something for $10,000, but I back away and say, "I'll give you this for $2,000." If you found enough value to be interested at $10,000, what is the likelihood you'll pull out your checkbook and write a check for $2,000? Very high.

Get your market involved in taking action while you're persuading. Have them commit to doing small, inconsequential things. "Are you most interested in this? Click on this," and then the website changes. Small, inconsequential steps get people to take other actions, whether in person or on the web. Set up situations or scenarios that they can agree on. Tell pieces of the story that they can empathize with. Use graphics, brochures, audio, or any other props that you need to demonstrate your point and no more. People go overboard with this stuff. Use all you need to sell, then stop. Keep your audience's attention focused on you. You want them focused on you if you're selling in person. You want them focused on moving forward to the next steps if you're selling in writing.

If you're selling in person, focus on your nonverbal language. Make sure that you're an honest communicator. Fifty percent of what people use to identify whether you're being truthful or not comes from your face. Some people should not be on video, not because they're ugly, but because they don't come across as honest. People look at your face and make those decisions. There are high return rates for video products by people who don't appear honest.

Use good facial expressions. Smile often. I'm smiling inside all the time, I'm a happy person, but I'm not a person who thinks to smile at people all the time. I have a constant reminder to myself to smile. In my talks I even mark out the points where I should smile at people. It makes them happy; it makes them feel good. Take the time to smile; use good facial gestures. Also, smile while you're writing.

Ask or tell your audience what you want them to do. Present your request in a way that is consistent with their expectations and your presentation. Project confidence. Expect them to do something. A big part of selling and influence is expecting the audience to take the next step because it would be insane if they didn't.

Install the reticular activator. A reticular activator is something that you are going to see or experience in the future that's going to remind you of something in the past. Say that I tell you that the next time you read a headline that starts out with, "Three things that you'll never know about . . . ," it's going to remind you that this is a hypnotic headline. Later, when you see a headline like that, you'll say, "Oh, yeah, that's right. That's a hypnotic headline." I'm setting a reticular activator for something that I know will happen to you in the future.

Columbia House, Columbia Records' now defunct mail-order record club, used this technique very effectively. They would say, "Look in your mailbox for this item."

When you saw it, it would remind you of the whole process that got you to sign up for the club in the first place.

Future-pace what you want your audience to experience. Set them in the future after having acted on something you've had them do. Remember, nothing can happen until you've already taken an action in your mind. Get them to take that action in their mind. Pace it into the future by saying, "This is what will have happened because you took this action."

If you want to draw a large group of people to you after an event, tell an engaging or emotional story, and leave off just before you finish. If you want to suck away the audience from another speaker, all you have to do is leave off the ending to your story. The audience can't pay attention to the next person. They've got to get to you to hear the rest of that story. This is a powerful tool.

By using these principles every step of the way, you'll be able to build a tremendous power of persuasion. Use them at all appropriate opportunities. Initiate the law of reciprocation any way you can. People who market on the Internet do this better than anyone else. They utilize free reports, free e-books, free audio, free teleconferences. These are tremendously powerful.

Use transference whenever possible. Recruit or meet people who already have influence or authority over the people you want to sell to. Get them to introduce you, endorse you, give testimonials for you. Reinforce your authority or expert status any chance you get through appropriate interactions and in ways that benefit your audience.

Build on beliefs and on the desire to believe. Reinforce current or long-held beliefs. Tie in your own beliefs with theirs. If you reinforce someone's belief, and you tie yours to it, you're taking advantage of nonverbal transference.

Cause your audience to be curious and engage you in more detailed conversations and questions. You want them to want more information. Use the scarcity principle to reinforce why taking action now is imperative.

The principles of human influence can be applied in person and in writing, on the web, on the television, radio, or in just about any area. If you take these ideas and apply them, you'll move audiences to take dramatic action with you.

For further reading, I would call your attention to Robert Cialdini's *Influence* and Kevin Hogan's book *The Psychology of Influence*. I also recommend a number of books by Steven Pinker. Just pick any book on the brain by Steven Pinker, take a look at it, and you'll understand the cognitive neuroscience of the brain more deeply.

7

My Twenty-One Point Secret Checklist

At this point, I'm going to go through the twenty-one-point secret checklist that I use to improve my copy. To me, this is worth hundreds of thousands of dollars. It was created by a multimillion-dollar copywriter in Switzerland named Christian Godefroy. He wrote a book called *How to Write Letters That Sell*, which is unfortunately out of print and very hard to find.

1. The Headline
Obviously the first thing is the headline. A good headline can make or destroy sales. If your headline conveys a

benefit of interest to your key audience, your letter has a massive chance of being read. Use a weak headline, and your letter dies.

The headline is not going to guarantee a sale. At this point, we're just stopping people—hopefully, the appropriate crowd for whatever we're offering.

Here are some examples of both effective and ineffective headlines:

Warning: don't throw this postcard away.

The word "warning" works almost every time. It's an eye-catcher. The writer already knows what my trance is: I want to throw the postcard away. They're saying, "Don't throw it away." All right, I'll give you one second to tell me what this is all about.

Here's a different kind of example: *Are you ready yet to achieve the web?*

Two things bother me about this headline. First, it asks a question. I love questions, but this is a yes or no question. I can easily say yes or no to that. Furthermore, it confuses me. I don't know what it means "to achieve the web." It's broken rapport with me. It's not building curiosity at all, because there's no foundation that says, "Joe, read this, because you're going to learn much more about this subject."

At last! The secret to making real money in your HVAC business guaranteed.

I think that's a good headline. It has the basics. It's targeted towards people who know what *HVAC* means, which is *heating, ventilation, and air conditioning*. It's going to stand out from everything else that's being mailed to that audience, so I think tit calls out the right audience. It's engaging. You could find this kind of headline all over the place among the marketing audiences on the Internet. But my guess is that you won't find it in the HVAC industry.

Who else wants to know how to successfully market themselves as a therapist?

I think this is clear and benefit-driven. The "who else?" headline does work. Again, in the marketing industry, people may have seen too much of it. But if it's going to an audience that doesn't see those headlines, it's going to be fresh.

Here's your foolproof, paint-by-numbers, connect-the-dots, step-by-step, shortcut success system that generates more traffic leads and prospects for your business.

I would look at this as a ruthless editor. I'd be asking myself, "Can I make that four-line headline into two lines?" Here's an alternative: *Here's your paint-by-numbers system that generates more traffic leads and prospects for your business.*

Then you could write a secondary headline underneath it that says something like, *Here's a foolproof, connect-the-dots way to generate leads.* "Foolproof" complements "paint-by-numbers": they're not redundant, and they do go together.

In short, you could break this headline up into two: one big line that's pulling them in, and a second line that could be almost exactly the same. I would make the top one bigger and the next one smaller, and then go into the smaller text. I'm sliding them in visually.

I look at headlines as billboards. If you drive down the highway and a billboard has a lot of text on it, you can't read it, and I think that's pointless. I think they're wasting their money. There needs to be something that communicates the key message right away, that makes you want to read more and know more so that you make the phone call.

2. Headline Design

I'm tired of seeing websites that are using a lot of odd fonts or are mixing fonts. There are thousands of fonts. I've heard that almost 100,000 different fonts are available, but we don't want all of them. For direct marketing campaigns, there are only two that you need. One is **Times Roman,** a serif font that practically all of the print media use. We all grew up on it, so we're used to it. The other one is a sans serif font. Some alternatives are **Helvetica, Arial,** and **Tahoma.**

Another point: Sans serif fonts like Arial are easier to read onscreen. Times Roman and other serif fonts are easier to read in print. Times Roman, however, is found in many authoritative publications, so when you see it, part of your mind goes, "This is authoritative."

Is the headline design inviting? Is it easy to read? Because the campaign here is to get them to read your letter. If it looks difficult, it does not look inviting. If it's not approachable, they're not going to read it.

Fancy type won't get you more readers. Use as simple a design as possible. Handwriting font could work. In fact, anything that is readable could work. Just don't get artsy. Simple and direct is best. Again, follow the pros. Use what famous copywriters use to write their sales letters: simple headline design.

3. Promise/Curiosity

If the headline creates curiosity while promising a benefit, you have a winner. Put some sizzle in that headline. Every good headline should arouse curiosity while promising something the reader wants. (Again, think of your reader.)

Curiosity is probably my favorite hypnotic technique. Why? Because it opens the mind to receive more. When I ask you, "What was Homer Simpson's middle name?" I activate the curiosity button in you. Even though you don't really care, your curiosity is sharpened. "What was Homer Simpson's middle name?" you ask yourself. You'll not rest until I tell you. During the time you are wondering what the answer is, your mind is open for me to install whatever I want.

Here's an example: *Introducing the new American land rush. How to buy real estate with government money.* That's a how-to; it's a strong promise of something that people want.

This example also has a preliminary headline: *Now even first-time homebuyers can use government grants to buy and own real estate investments.* This was written to play to search engines. I have written copy that was designed more for search engines than for the reader looking at the website. Such headlines are fed with keywords that the target audience might have been putting in. (Search engines, incidentally, are only keyed to the first fifty words up at the very top of the site.)

One issue: you can get a penalty for overoptimizing your site and having it mentioned too many times. Some experts recommend limiting yourself to two or three different keywords. Beyond that, by my understanding, is overkill.

Another tip: if you're focusing on web traffic only, use a blog to drive it. You can drive any search term or phrase that you want to with a blog. It will hit within twenty-four hours, and you're going to be in the top fifteen or twenty in Google for just about any search term you do. You just link it back to your site, and that will drive people there.

4. Letterhead/Logo

Your letterhead or logo should fit the product or service. If you look unprofessional, you won't be taken seriously. To put more emphasis on your headline, you can move your letterhead to the bottom of the last page of your sales letter. But you should have a letterhead, as it helps convey trust in you and your offer.

Online, your letterhead is your banner. Again, you can put your banner at the top of your site, letting your headline get all the attention at the top of your email.

Kevin Hogan, whose book I mentioned in the previous chapter, is a dear friend and a student. Once he and I sat in his booth at the National Guild of Hypnotists and made a homemade DVD in which we asked each other hard questions. One thing he said was eye-opening to me: the human mind goes through a buying cycle that lasts about eight minutes.

Kevin also said, "At the top of your website, you should have an order button." It needs to be, not right at the top, where your headline is, but within the first few paragraphs, somewhere on the right or on the left. Somewhere in there, you should have an order button, because some people are going to make an instant decision. Others are going through the eight-minute buying cycle in their head, thinking, "Should I buy, or should I not buy?

Should I buy, should I not buy?" During that cycle, they need to have the opportunity to buy.

That led me to ask Kevin, "Does that mean that all sales letters should be able to be read in under eight minutes?"

"No. Absolutely not," he said. "People are going to keep reading every word if they're interested at all. They'll keep reading every word, and they'll make their decision at the end. We've got to keep in mind that human brain tends to go through this cycle. We need to give them the ability to buy during that cycle."

5. The Opening Paragraph

Make it captivating. I like to begin with questions or a story. Anything to snare readers. Keep in mind that people are busy. They don't care at all about you. Your letter has to trip them. It has to interrupt them. A great headline and a great opening line can grab their attention. I spend a lot of time on the openings of my letters. How long? Maybe days.

Advertising legend Bruce Barton said that a lot of people start writing things before they start saying things. I've done this too. You start writing, and the first page may not be usable at all. It was almost like your brain dump to clear the way. It was just getting out whatever was on your mind. This material may be useful, but it may not be. I have found more often than not that the first page of a sales letter, a website, or a book can almost always be deleted without anybody missing it.

That's a clue to the rewriting stage. Consider the weak areas—the first page, the first chapter, sometimes the first paragraph in new sections. Are you just warming up? You're starting to tell somebody what you want to tell them, but you're not telling them the meat.

Here is a million-dollar tip: good copywriters know how to use bullets. They're visually attractive, and they usually lead your mind to some of the things you're thinking about.

Another million-dollar secret: change statements into questions. Instead of saying, *"Here's how to get more good customers in a month than you've gotten all year,"* write, *"How can you get more good customers in a month than you have gotten all year?"* It's still a bullet point, but there's a question mark. They can't answer.

Another example: *"Be able to at least double your Yellow Pages response."* I would change that to *"How can you at least double your Yellow Pages response?"* This is a minor thing, but it's powerful in the end result. These bulleted points now become engagers. The reader is going into a hypnotic trance. They're thinking, "How can I get a year's worth of good customers in a month?" "How can I at least double my Yellow Pages response?" They're starting to wonder. You're also taking out the critical attack. You're not saying you have the answer. You're giving yourself more airtime to build rapport with the reader before they come up with objections. It's a very soft approach. You're also implying a hidden benefit, because you're leading up to the fact that you do have an answer. That's very hypnotic. At the back of their mind, they're thinking, "He must know."

6. The Offer

What are you selling? What's the deal? Once you have the attention of your reader, you have to keep it. Your reader will want to know right away—almost instantly—what your offer is. Tell him.

Many people judge whether or not they're going to continue reading by the price of the item, so they want to see the price fairly quickly. They get to it and say, "OK. It's under $200. I buy things under $200. I'll read this and see if this piques my interest enough, but if it's $1,400, I'm not going to read it, because I'm not going to buy, no matter what."

I've gone back and forth on that over the years. I used to think that you needed to bury the price at the end to get people to read all of the copy. Then Carl Galletti, another great copywriter, said to have the price up front, because there are people who need to know if the item is in their budget range.

Of course, when you're talking about the Internet, everything changes all the time, so everything has to be tested. The great god in all of this is testing.

To go back to Kevin Hogan's eight-minute cycle, the reader is oscillating between saying, "No, forget this," and "Yes, I want this." You need to spell out your offer early on in your copy, so people can insert these facts into their heads.

You've engaged your target audience; you've stopped them. Now you need to be able to tell them what this is all about fairly quickly, although maybe not immediately.

7. Advantages

Why buy? If your reader is still with you, they will want to know the advantages of having your product or service. This is a good place to paint a story, as Robert Collier suggested. Get your reader feeling what it would be like to have or do what you suggest. Give them emotional and logical reasons to buy whatever you are selling. Pile on the advantages.

8. Positive Language

Be enthusiastic, upbeat. Show your excitement. This is the secret trick of John Caples, one of the most famous copywriters of all time. We copywriters pump ourselves up. We get excited, and we show that excitement in our letters. This only works if you sincerely believe in what you are offering. If you don't, your reader will smell a rat. Get readers saying yes through questions that make them agree with you. Bring good news.

9. Emphasis on Important Passages

Attract attention to important phrases or paragraphs by using subheads throughout your letter. This breaks it up to make it easier to read. You might also underline key passages or use caps (sparingly). Sometimes handwriting in the margin of your letters can emphasize important sections. Dan Kennedy is known for his busy letters. He does that intentionally. It draws attention to certain parts of the letter and makes it look unusual as well as personal.

My longtime friend and client John Du Cane runs a website for his publishing company, Dragon Door Publications. One time, he sent out a postcard that was incredibly busy. It was so hard to read that I had to put on higher-strength reading glasses to read the handwriting. It was a very busy card. The only reason that I even tried to read it is that it said "Dragon Door Publications" in the corner, so I knew who it was coming from. There was a built-in relationship and built-in rapport, and I was curious. I emailed John and asked, "How did that card do for you? Because it was pretty hard to read." He said, "This card pulled more book orders than anything else I've done in years."

"Why do you think that was?"

"The handwriting made everybody curious. It made them invest some time in reading it."

The card was very busy, but I was able to pull out what it was all about. The call to action was very clear: "Call this 1-800 number to get the book." I called and ordered it. I know John. I could have gotten one for free. I fought to read the whole thing, but I bought.

The next thing John did was send out a giant postcard. I think he got this idea from me. I told him how great this very busy postcard was, but a lot of people probably didn't see it. I jokingly said, "You ought to send out a giant card that says, 'If you couldn't read my last one, you should be able to read this one.'" He sent out a huge card that said that.

10. The Egometer

I love looking for the egometer. Is your letter or website focusing on the reader? Focus on your reader. The more you can use the magic word *you*, the more your reader will like it. A good test is to count the number of times you used the word *you* in your sales letter. The more *you's*, the better. Notice how many times I used the word *you* in just this paragraph. It helps involve you in my writing and makes you feel as if I am writing to you and only you. Appeal to your reader's ego.

11. Readability

Short sentences of simple words will help make your letter hypnotic. You're writing for people who want things simple. Don't confuse them or try to impress them. Be conversational.

You might use the famous formula at the back of Rudolph Flesch's book *The Complete Guide to Readable Writing*. He has a readability formula there: you go in, count your sentences, count the syllables, and you can find out the grade level of your writing.

You want your copy to be easy to read. You also want its structure to be easy.

12. Structure

Your letter should look inviting. If you have long paragraphs of dense type, it won't. Only some of your readers will read your letter word for word. Others will skim it. Structure your letter to please both.

Imagine that you're opening up two different kinds of books. One has wall-to-wall text and the other has dialogue, short sentences, and short paragraphs. Which one would you read?

13. Personal Aspect

Your letter should read as if you wrote it only for me. Write your sales letter to just one person. Write it to a friend. Later, take out your friend's name. You'll have a personal letter that should feel as if it had been written for whoever picked it up.

Don't be afraid to show your own personality. Tell me why you love your product or service in a way that interests me and makes me want it too.

14. Interest Boosters

Throughout your letter or website, there should be interest boosters plugged in to keep people reading. These are everything from engaging subheads to incomplete sentences to questions to story beginnings. Do you know what I mean? Actually, I've snuck in an interest booster just now, with a question: "Do you know what I mean?" You're finding ways to keep people focused on every word of your copy. Make sense?

15. Page Breaks

I like to break paragraphs to force people to keep reading. I might get near the end of a page and write something like, "And now for the biggest . . ." and leave it there. The reader then has to turn the page over to finish the sentence. People don't like unfinished *anything*. They'll turn the page over.

There's some argument about this subject. Some prefer a long direct-mail page that is not broken at all. Again, the only real way to answer the question for yourself is through testing.

16. Proof

Back up your claims with testimonials and a strong guarantee. Writing sales letters is making pleas to strangers. You need to convince them that you are legit. Do that with testimonials—quotes from previous customers. I'm a big fan of testimonials. Add all you can.

Add a powerful guarantee. Make it even more powerful by putting all the risk on you. Instead of "Guaranteed for 30 days," say, "Guaranteed for life!" If you believe in your product or service, why wouldn't you give a strong guarantee? Show confidence in your offer.

Other means of proof are evidence and statistics. You want to convince your audience so that they know your product or service will work for them.

17. Conclusion

Is there a call to action in your letter? Are you wrapping it up by asking your reader to do something in particular? Tell them what you want them to do.

I also like to put a spell on readers. I sometimes end my letters with a question such as: "Will this program work for you? You'll never know unless you reply right now, before it's too late." The idea here is to leave them ready to act. Tell them what to do. Say, "Call me" if you want them to call you.

18. Gifts

Give. Your readers are selfish. They won't act easily. You have to offer an ethical bribe to encourage action. Once I received a sales letter about a new vitamin supplement. Along with the offer, they said they would send me a free workout radio if I replied within ten days. That "free" radio cast a hypnotic spell on me.

This is called the *psychology of the second interest*: some people will buy your product in order to get what you're offering for free along with it. This technique works. Use it.

19. The P.S.

I've renamed the P.S. as "powerful statement." It is your opportunity to condense and convey a persuasive piece of information.

20. Number of Lines per Paragraph

Your paragraphs should be very short: less than six lines each. People are busy and want things quick and simple. Even if you are writing to CEOs, your letter should be breezy.

This goes back to being inviting and easy to read. Online, you will often find paragraphs that are just one sentence.

21. Dynamism

The overall look and feel of your sales letter or website need to convey excitement.

Your letter should move, flow, run, sprint. There should be urgency—a sense of "wow!" If you have a product you believe in, that dynamism should be there naturally.

The Eleven Words

You'll remember that I said there were three words that I could say to you that would make you give me all your money. When my grandfather came to this country from Italy around 1910, he did not speak one word of English. He learned three words. With those three words, he was able to get anything he wanted. They were, "Stick 'em up."

I also said that there were eight words that would cause you never to worry about money again. Inspirational writer Mike Dooley put them on his website, TUT. com (for "think useful thoughts"). One day he sent out an email, a message from the universe, that said, "I understand you've been worried about money. Well, let me remove your money worries once and for all." He said these words: "You never have to worry about money again."

Some people immediately get it. Some people say, "What?" The point is, worrying about money doesn't bring you any money. Worrying about money is a psychological tactic we've learned to use to motivate ourselves to make money. But it doesn't work.

The note from the universe says you never have to worry about money. Done deal. It's over. You don't have to worry about money. You've still got to work for it, earn it, and write hypnotic copy. But you don't have to worry about money.

8

My Three-Part Hypnotic Marketing Strategy

In this chapter, I'm going to explore a three-part marketing strategy that I've been using with clients. This is a very expensive strategy. People have paid thousands of dollars just to have it described to them.

This hypnotic three-step marketing strategy works. It integrates all I have done over the decades. You all know I've written several books, recorded a lot of audios, done many speaking engagements. I've even created software.

On his deathbed in 1891, P. T. Barnum said, "I am indebted to the press of the United States for almost

every dollar which I possess." He was one of the wealthiest people in the world. You still know his name today,
even though he's been dead for over 125 years. He said
this on his deathbed to a friend, telling him, "If you follow
my methods, you will not fail."

Hypnotic Publicity

Step one in this three-step formula, which is a step that
Barnum used a lot, is called *hypnotic publicity*. The media
is hungry for news. If there's anything that I see marketers
not doing enough of—especially Internet marketers—it's
using the press. They're not doing media relations. They're
not sending out news.

You may not know this, but 80 percent of what you
read in a newspaper was planted there by somebody who
wanted you to see it. Somebody sent it out in the form of
a news release. Or an ad agency was hired to write it and
send it out.

One way you can use the media is to tie your business to current news. For example, you can make predictions about your business. I've had great success with this
technique.

You can also run a survey. The media loves surveys.
If you've ever noticed, newspapers like *USA Today* have
surveys right on the front at the bottom.

Those surveys never really have that much news. If you run another survey, you'll get a different result from the one that was just published. But surveys look like news. The papers love them.

Humor wins in the media too. I'm going to show you a way that humor has been used to get media coverage nationwide.

Another major point: you want to send your message out as a one-sheet news release.

Here are some headlines I've seen. As I've already emphasized, your headlines are the most important thing. They're trying to get you to click through to a larger story.

One of the most powerful psychological motivators is curiosity. Would you like to know how curiosity works? All right. *What's the next trend in cars?* I love answering questions that you can't answer without reading the rest of the story. It's a tease, making you want to learn more.

Start thinking about how you could apply this to your business, whether it's online or offline.

Here's another one. *Quiz: life's most critical decisions.* The media loves quizzes. You can tie a quiz into whatever you're offering.

Others: *Is your mate stashing cash? Where to live if you hate taxes. Switching cell plans? What to avoid. Champagne dates, beer budget.* All of these are actual headlines.

These are engaging teases. You can send them to the media as a headline with a short story underneath, which makes people want to know more. You can see how these headlines make you want to know more.

Now here's the hypnotic trick, the $25,000 twist to this first step. Most people who send out news releases leave this part out. They send out news releases that are very egocentric. They'll send out something that says, "I have a new book," or "I have a new product," or "I have a new person working for me," or "I have a new company." That is soft news: the papers might run it in a couple of lines in some section that nobody ever looks at, if they run it at all.

You want to get more coverage, so you want to create something that's much more engaging along the lines of the headlines we just saw.

The hypnotic trick to making all of this work is to give part of the news in your release, with the rest of the story at your website. This is all about integrated marketing. I'm not just telling you to send out a news release, because I think that alone could be a mistake. You want to send out a news release that only gives part of the news. You want to give them the seed of a story and let the media complete it. They'll call you to get the rest of the information, or they'll go to your website for it.

You want to plant the seed. Do you get that? If you're giving tips, offer five tips, with the other five on your website.

You can even do this with something quite arcane. Say you're promoting a transcription service. You could write, "How to choose a transcriptionist." You might want to have ten tips, or seven, or fifteen. Change the headline accordingly. But only give half of them of them in your release. Provide a website link where they can get the rest.

You don't control the media, but you're trying to befriend them. You're trying to help them so they will help you. If they plant the story and say, "Here are some of the tips: if you want all of them, go to this website," that is a major win for you.

As we've already discovered, curiosity is powerful. I encourage you to be outrageous. Think of the wildest things. Stretch your imagination to come up with things that you think won't work. Have a glass of wine and free-associate. Get together with friends and brainstorm. Laugh at everything. The ones you laugh at the hardest will probably be the ones that will really work.

I once bought a mermaid on eBay. It was half fish and half wax, and it smelled terrible. It probably began life as a sea horse, but someone with a Barnum touch turned into a mermaid and sold it online—to me.

I had a wild idea. I knew there is a lot of traffic on eBay for superstars: Madonna, Britney Spears, Elvis. What if I somehow created a superstar mermaid and put it up on eBay?

I went to my wife at the time, who did a lot of graphic work, and asked, "Can you take a picture of our mermaid and then do some kind of graphic work to the picture and make it look like a superstar?"

As we looked at the mermaid and were playing with ideas, she said, "Maybe an Elvis mermaid." We created a photograph of an original Elvis mermaid and put it up on eBay. People typing in *Elvis* were now seeing something called an Elvis mermaid. The few that were typing in *mermaid* were now seeing something called an Elvis mermaid. I also mentioned P. T. Barnum.

I didn't think I'd make any money from this. I wasn't doing it to sell the photograph. I was doing it to drive traffic to the spot on eBay where I mentioned my website: "For more information about Joe, P. T. Barnum, and mermaids, go to Joe's website, MrFire.com."

I had no idea if this would work or not. I was prepared not to tell anybody if it didn't. I listed the mermaid. Immediately there was traffic—within seconds. Nobody was bidding on it, which I didn't care about, because it was just a photograph. But I was getting traffic from that going to my website, MrFire. Then a radio station called me up. It was one of these morning zoo shows, which are very disrespectful, but they're fun. They wanted to interview me about the Elvis mermaid.

I went on two shows, which caused traffic to go to my website (I saw the spike right afterward). I also saw the new subscriptions that came into my website. People wanted to sign on for this wild man who creates Elvis mermaids. The radio station bid and won the Elvis mermaid. They put it in their lobby so people could see it. After they got it, they were pretty unhappy with it, but that's a different story.

This wasn't a big success story, but it's an odd one, and I wanted you to read it to get an idea of what you can do.

Think about what you are selling, what your market is. Think about the problems you are solving with your product. Create news around it, or even tie it to current news.

I wrote a news release quite a while ago. The headline: *Who's going to crack next? How to tell if you are someone you love is about to snap.* This was for a book, but I did not say "new book" in the headline. Nor did I say it anywhere in the first couple of paragraphs. A new book is not news to the media; tens of thousands are published every year. If you say, "I have a new book," they'll say, "So what? Who cares?"

You have to put your book in context. This one was by a mental health expert. It was on solving mental health problems. He created a screening test, which I did not give in the news release but told him to put on his website. You see the difference: if we gave this story to the media and they ran with it, they would run all of it. But if you give the website and say, "You can find the quiz there," they'll have to visit the site.

This is how I shape this three-step hypnotic marketing formula. This first step involves publicity, but the second step involves websites. I'm trying to create a way for you to develop publicity that drives people to your website. This is how they're overlapping.

How do you get in the news? Here's an example: toilet paper. Marketer John Zappa and a friend of his came up with this idea on their own after listening to my audio program *The Power of Outrageous Marketing*. Their wild idea for using toilet paper to make fun of current news got them national and even international media attention. Printed on the toilet paper are ticker symbols of stocks that lost 95 to 99 percent of their value.

This is using the humor. John did it just for publicity, not to make money, although it did make money in just a few weeks. He had bulk orders for this product that he wasn't prepared for. It's the power of your intention and your passion. Can you just let go?

John says he never would have predicted that his biggest customers would have been the people in the financial community who got their clients to lose money on these crappy stocks. They bought it to give to them. "Sorry, I lost all your money, Bob, but here's a present. Here's some toilet paper."

Moreoever, this was tied into a current event. The stock market had just taken a dump. You turn a negative into a positive, add some humor to it, and dare to say what nobody else is willing to say. You'll get a response. Incidentally, the paper sold for $9.95 a roll.

The Hypnotic Website

Step one is publicity: the news release sends people to your website. Step two is the hypnotic website. Your site should complete the news story by, for example, giving the rest of your tips.

Make your site content-rich so people will want to return and want to hear from you. My website, MrFire .com, gets swamped with heavy traffic all the time in part because it is a huge, content-rich site. Create lots of content.

With this strategy, the first step is publicity, which leads people to go to your website for the rest of the content. When they're there, getting the content that they came for, there's other relevant content to keep them there. Hopefully it is so fascinating to them that they will sign up for your news bulletins.

That's why your site should also provide a way for people to give you their email addresses. There should be some way for them to sign up. Say, "If you would like to get weekly, monthly, or occasional news bulletins from us concerning this subject, just give us your email address."

Here's an example. I was at home. I was reading this magazine. I saw a news story that intrigued me. It was about a site selling stupid things like whoopee cushions. It was actually called stupid.com. I think it's a brilliant site. That's where I bought the vibrating pen that I mentioned earlier.

Now I saw this article in a magazine. Somebody planted that article; it was not an advertisement. Please note the difference here. The news releases you're sending out are getting you free coverage—free space in newspapers, magazines, on radio, on TV. You pay for advertising. I'm not against advertising. It definitely works, but it's very expensive. Most of the time when I work with people, I tell them, "Let's do the street-smartest approach. Let's not spend money, or at least as little as we have to."

Now you see how the hypnotic formula works. Step one: send out a news release with a reason embedded in it to drive traffic to your website. The media may not even notice that you've tricked them into sending their readers to your site.

Step two: your website, where people get the rest of the story.

Step three is your emails, which I will discuss next.

I remember sending out a news release on my P. T. Barnum book. It said something like, "Are P. T. Barnum's methods for success valid today?" I listed the top ten things that P. T. Barnum did that you can do today. I didn't see any response right away.

One night, a few months later, I started getting phone calls, faxes, emails from people congratulating me. I had no idea on what. Later I found out that A&E's *Biography*—a very respected, well-watched show—had created a new documentary on Barnum. At the end, the host held up one book and only one book. He said these exact words: "Are P. T. Barnum's methods for success valid today?" He held up the book, showed it, and then said a few words about the book.

I couldn't believe it. My book sold out overnight. It was one of my first best-sellers for which I didn't implement any strategy. I had sent out a news release. It was one of my first tastes of how a news release drives traffic to a website. The great bulk of the sales were from Amazon. My book was at 2 million in sales rank, and it shot up to 33 within an hour. I was stunned.

The Hypnotic Email

Step three is sending out your emails. When people come to your site, get their email addresses and use them to build relationships. I really work hard on this.

I was having lunch once with Mark Joyner, author of *MindControlMarketing.com*. He asked me, "Does anybody read your email beside you? Do you have any buffers?"

"No," I said. "I read all my email."

"Every one of them that comes in?"

"Yes."

"That's why."

"That's why what?"

"That's why you get such an incredible response from your email list."

Mark has a mailing list with a million names. He can send out a mailing for a product to his list that he's endorsing to a million names. I will send one out to my list, which was just in the tens of thousands—very small by comparison. I will get more responses than him.

It's not the size of the list that matters. It's the relationship. If your readers really trust you, and you say, "I have found something that I think is phenomenal, and it's going to really help your particular business," they will buy it. That's based on trust.

You're getting these emails to build relationships. Telling stories is one of my favorite things to do as a way of communicating in copy. Offering tips is another.

I'm building my email list, and I'm urging you to build an email list. Don't just bombard them with sales messages, though. I send a lot of email out, but I work incredibly hard to make it relevant to my readers. Apparently it works, because almost nobody unsubscribes: maybe one or two people per week. The list just keeps growing and getting bigger. I am working hard not to just hit them with sales. I'm offering them tips that I've come across. Or I mention or create a free e-book is relevant. Relevancy is so important. I'm not just giving nonsense to these people. I don't send them jokes unless I think they're the top ten marketing jokes.

If you have jokes pertaining to your particular product or service or industry, send them out. Write fifty. Send out the top ten as a news release, with the rest on the website. People read those ten jokes. The link to the website is there for the rest of them. Then the website also has a place for them to sign up for a weekly joke or other news or tips.

This formula works. This is the hypnotic marketing strategy.

When people go to your site, should they go to a special landing page, or should they go to the home page? I recommend a special landing page, with links for your home page over on the corner.

Offer specials. When I came out with my software, the Hypnotic Writing Wizard, we were testing prices. How much should we charge? I didn't know, so I made something up. I'm a great believer in making things up. Initially the product didn't sell fantastically. Then we came out with a special that said, "If you buy the Hypnotic Writing Wizard between Christmas and the end of the year, you can have it for $79." Originally we were selling it for $299. We sold four times as many programs in those few days than in the four months previous. Part of this was a matter of testing the price. Part of it was

offering a special with a good reason for it: an end of the
year sale.

Give freebies. I love to give people e-books, and I love
to get them. Again, it has to be relevant. I give away the
e-book of *Spiritual Marketing*. I tell anybody who has the
PDF that they can sell it or give it away; they can do whatever they like with it.

Part of my motivation is coming from the goodness
of my heart. I believe in my heart that this book makes a
difference to people. I get emails every day from people all
over the world who've read the book. They say their lives
have changed because of it. The moves me and aston-
ishes me and baffles me even. I thought, "If it's making
that much of a difference, I'll just give it away." The giving
principle works.

Bob Serling, who's another great marketing mind and
copywriter, came up with a book called *How to Position or
Reposition Any Product or Service for Maximum Sale*. He
wrote to me and said, "If you'd like to have this book and
give it to your list between now and Christmas, I'll give
you the link that they can use, and they can download it
for free." Normally, it sells for $29.

Why was Bob willing to do that for me? If you go to
that link, you're on his website. It was free viral promotion for his site. In effect, he got me to promote it. People
go to his site. The first thing they see is, "Yes, you can have

the book in a minute. How about subscribing to my news-letter?" This is how he built up his subscription list.

Why did I send his book out? For a gift. It makes me look good. It's also going out at Christmas. All of this amounts to win-win-wins. This entire strategy is designed to be a win-win-win. It's a very positive, even healing experience for everybody involved.

Viral marketing works this way: if people like it, they're going to wonder what else I wrote. I've written a lot of other things, most of which are for sale. If they get a freebie and like it, they might buy some of my other products. I'm a great believer in giving away freebies.

Again, all of this is open to experimentation, and I want you to experiment with what you're doing. I sent out an email that I now call my tough love letter. This is for the program *Beyond Positive Thinking*. It is a truly fantastic program. It's based on the work of Dr. Robert Anthony, who wrote a book with that title. When I was struggling and striving, I was reading his books and studying his tapes. That material made a difference to my life.

I didn't know where Dr. Anthony was. I even thought he was dead. Later he surfaced. He sent me an email from Australia saying he'd read a free copy of *Spiritual Marketing* and telling me how much he liked the book. Eventually we coauthored a book called *Spiritual Marketing in Action*.

I sent out an email that I didn't want people to ignore or forget. I told them in the opening paragraph, "This is the greatest material ever recorded in history on achieving results in your life. If you don't get the CD set right now, you should not be on my email list."

That was a very bold move, but in my gut, I knew that was the stance I needed to take, because my belief was with it. In the end, only two people unsubscribed. A few wrote me and said, "I can't believe you told me you would unsubscribe me if I don't buy your book." But that was not what I said. I just said you should unsubscribe; I didn't say that I would unsubscribe you.

I got this idea from the late Stuart Wilde, a metaphysical wild man. At one point, he came out with a book and sent out an email that said, "This is my latest book. You're on my list because you want to know about the things I do. You should buy my book. If you don't buy my book, I'm unsubscribing you." He wasn't polite like me. He didn't merely suggest that you should unsubscribe. He said, "If you don't buy my book, I'm unsubscribing you." I bought his book because I wanted to stay on his list to see what this Gonzo man was going to come up with next.

A week or so later, Stuart came out with a follow-up email that said, "A whole bunch of you people wrote to me, and you were angry. I really pushed your button." He cleverly turned it around: "Instead of letting me push your button, that's something for you to look at. Why do you have so much anger within you?" He used that as an opportunity for clearing within yourself. More people bought the book.

Then Stuart came out with another email that said, "A lot of you have asked, was I kidding about whether I would unsubscribe you or not?" He said, "Yes, I was." The next line said, "No, I wasn't. Love, Stuart." He left you wondering. Was he kidding? Was he not kidding? Was he going to take you off the list? Was he not going to take you off the list? What was going on with this guy?

I adapted Stuart's very tough formula. I thought, "I'm kind of a nice guy. I don't want to say I'm going to unsubscribe people. I'll just say you shouldn't be on my list."

In the end, the sales of my book went through the roof (except for the two people who unsubscribed, which was fine with me).

Specifics are another tip. Make your emails very specific. I wrote material advertising an e-class on how to teach your own e-classes. It's full of specific details like, "I'm looking for ten people on my email list who would like to personally learn from me how to make $5,000 to $15,000 in just three weeks teaching their very own e-class."

There's my offer. Then I go in, and I give more specifics: "I taught Yanik Silver how to make $18,298.50 on his first e-class. He's made $90,000 teaching e-classes." This email is incredibly persuasive because it's so specific. That's an example of what you can send out.

Let me sum up the formula that I've been talking about.

1. **Hypnotic publicity.** Send out a single news release with a link to your website. You plant the seed of a story. The rest of the story is on a website.

2. **Hypnotic website.** Complete the news story on your site. Have a means to collect email addresses. Maybe give them something, like an e-book, if they sign up for your email.

3. **Hypnotic email.** Send out relevant emails to build relationships.

Admittedly, I come out with some products that don't sell. One time I came out with an e-class on publicity. I thought that everybody in the universe would sign up for it and I would be turning people away. I worked very hard on the sales letter. I did everything I knew to do. I sent it out. Not one person signed up. None.

As Tom Cruise said, "I don't pretend to know what's going to make money." I never know what's going to work. I have certain hopes. I have certain intuitions. I'm trusting that either something is going to work or I'm going to learn from it. I just say to myself, "OK. That didn't work. I might try another time."

You may wonder if I do any offline marketing—such as postcards and sales letters—along with online marketing. I recommend integrated marketing, including direct mail.

I know people who are making $1.8 million a month on the Internet. I asked them, "Are you really doing that just on the Internet?" No. They're also sending out sales letters. They're sending out postcards. They're doing things that drive people to the Internet. They're using these things in concert.

9

Some Magical Lists

I have a list of words that are considered to be hypnotic:

- Announcing
- Fantastic
- Guaranteed
- Limited offer
- Revealing
- Super
- Wonderful
- Astonishing
- Fascinating
- Incredible
- Love
- Revolutionary
- Time-sensitive
- Exciting
- First
- Initial
- Powerful
- Special
- Unique
- Exclusive
- Free
- Improved
- Phenomenal
- Successful
- Urgent
- Breakthrough

You can create headlines just with these words. That's how powerful they are. But if you only do that, you'll end up with hype. However, if you take whatever you're trying to sell and you put in some of these words, you'll increase your connection with readers.

Hypnotic Phrases

Then there are hypnotic phrases, such as:

—*As you start reading the beginning of this article, you find yourself . . .*

—*As you sit there and read the beginning of this report, you start to feel . . .*

—*As you read every word of this report, you will become (amazed, stunned, etc.) at . . .*

—*As you analyze each word of this document, you will shortly feel a sense of (calmness, joy, etc.) . . .*

—*As you scan every word of this web page, you will begin to discover new ways of . . .*

—*After you read this short article, you will feel . . .*

—*Can you imagine . . .*

—*Picture yourself five years from now . . .*

—*Just picture . . .*

—*Just imagine . . .*

—*Remember when you were in high school . . .*

—*Imagine what it would be like if . . .*

—*Wouldn't it be amazing if . . .*

—And in those early years of existence . . .
—Imagine what it would be like if you could . . .
—See yourself . . .
—Remember the smell of . . .
—And you begin to notice . . .
—Do you remember hearing . . .
—Can you recall what an (insert word) feels like?

Tip: Use statements at the beginning of your writing that your prospects already know to be true. This creates trust right away. Trust leads to sales and gets people to do what you want them to do. For example:

—You probably know . . .
—You're intelligent enough to know . . .
—Of course you've heard that . . .
—Everyone knows . . .
—You probably already know this . . .
—Rare thinking people like you already know that . . .

These are hypnotic phrases. Weave them into your copy. They can be things like, *As you sit there and read the beginning of this report . . .* You lead them to feel what you want them to feel.

As you read every word of this report, you will become— amazed, stunned, and so on. *After you read this short article, you will feel—*how do you want them to feel? Put it in there.

Many of these activate the visual part of the brain. We think in pictures, so you want to activate and communicate with that part of people's brains.

Picture yourself five years from now . . . That's a beautiful one. If you're trying to sell something, get people to imagine what would it be like if they had it and where they would be in five years. Get them into that dream.

Remember when you were in high school. Imagine what it would be like if . . . Wouldn't it be amazing if . . . In those early years of existence . . . Do you see how these are props? Do you see how they can make your writing much easier?

Hypnotic Writing Is . . .

Here are some characteristics of hypnotic writing:

- Hypnotic writing is personal.
- Hypnotic writing speaks to you. It's active.
- Hypnotic writing has a lot of verbs in it. You won't find passive writing.
- Hypnotic writing is emotional. It taps into your feelings.
- Hypnotic writing is sensual. It will involve all of your senses through words and go into your mind.
- Hypnotic writing will command you to do something. After you read any piece of any copy, ask yourself what you want to do as a result. Usually there was some kind of command that maybe was effective and maybe wasn't.

- Hypnotic writing arouses curiosity.
- Hypnotic writing is also hidden. You don't usually see it. If you've written a piece of copy, you show it to somebody, and they say, "Wow, this is great writing!" it's not great writing. You want them to read it and say, "Where do I get that?" They don't know it's hypnotic writing. They just know they want the product.

Why People Buy

This list has been around for a long time. It gives twenty-six reasons why people buy:

- To make money
- To save money
- To save time
- To avoid effort
- To get more comfort
- To achieve greater cleanliness
- To attain fuller health
- To escape physical pain
- To gain praise
- To be popular
- To attract the opposite sex
- To conserve possessions
- To increase enjoyment
- To gratify curiosity
- To protect family
- To be in style
- To have or hold beautiful possessions
- To satisfy appetite
- To emulate others
- To avoid trouble
- To avoid criticism
- To be individual
- To protect reputation
- To take advantage of opportunities
- To have safety
- To make work easier

Tie whatever you are selling to one or more of these reasons.

Maslow Was Wrong

Here's a great headline: "Maslow Was Wrong." An Ohio State University professor, Steven Reiss, who wrote a book called *Who Am I?*, announced it with this news release. That is riveting.

Everybody worships Abraham Maslow. They say his hierarchy of needs explains the way that everybody operates. Reiss comes along and says Maslow was wrong. He says those needs have changed. We're in a different time. We're with different people. We're with different stresses. We have different goals and desires. Reiss developed a list of sixteen basic desires, which he describes in his book. To create hypnotic writing, you want to tag into some of these:

- Power
- Independence
- Curiosity
- Acceptance
- Order
- Saving
- Honor
- Idealism
- Social contact
- Family
- Status
- Vengeance
- Romance
- Eating
- Physical activity
- Tranquility

Here's a similar list of what people want:

- Health
- Time
- Money
- Popularity
- Improved appearance
- Security
- Praise from others
- Comfort
- Leisure
- Pride of accomplishment
- Advancement
- Business
- Social interests
- Enjoyment
- Self-confidence
- Personal prestige
- To be a good parents
- To be sociable

Again, your writing will be more hypnotic if you associate what you're trying to sell with these inbuilt desires.

A Headline Quiz

Let's take a little quiz. Look at two headlines for the same product, and decide which one is hypnotic.

1. *How to stop baldness from stopping you.*
2. *Solve your problem of baldness. Send for this free book today.*

The correct answer is 2. *Solve your problem of baldness.* *Solve* implies that you're going to get rid of your problem. *Free* is one of the power words mentioned above.

Here's another example: two headlines for the same product. Which of these is hypnotic?

1. *Only one cruise line gives you all these great vacation spots plus Bermuda.*
2. *Twenty years ago, the Chinese reserved this kind of treatment for presidents and kings.*

The correct answer is 1. It's is more hypnotic. It addresses what people want in a very clear way. With 2, you don't even know it's about a cruise. You might have missed it. The first one is direct. It speaks to what you're looking for, so it's more targeted.

In fact, the first got a 67 percent better response. Why? A clear benefit. You know at a glance what was being offered. If you're in the market for a cruise line, you're going to go with the one that says "cruise line."

When I first looked at this pair, I actually chose the second one. I thought, "That's kind of romantic—talking about twenty years ago." It sounded historic, and there's something intriguing in that. But if I were flipping through a magazine, I'd probably pass by this ad. If I were looking for a cruise line, I'd want to know which ad talks about the cruise line. The first headline speaks to a direct benefit.

Two more, again both for the same product:

1. *Introducing ProEdit, the world's smallest video production studio.*
2. *Two out, bottom of the ninth, you'd better catch it.*

Again, the first is the better one. Like the second one in the previous example, 2 is hidden. You don't know what it's about. You have to read the ad. It's better to be direct and speak to what people want.

Which of the following is more powerful, more hypnotic?

1. *Products you can stick with.*
2. *The company that sticks with you.*

Here too 1 is the better headline, because it's about you. With 2, the company talking about itself. But nobody really cares about what a company does for you. Some may think a company that sticks with you is going to be good because the company is saying, "I'm going to be reliable." But people are more concerned about the product.

Neither of these is a great headline, but this example illustrates a powerful point: people want to know what your *product* is going to do for them, not what your *company* is going to do for them.

Another pair of headlines for the same item:

1. *Products you can stick with.*
2. *A company that sticks with you.*

The big winner is 1. *Products you can stick with.* The reason? People care more about what they may get, not what you may offer. As for the other one, *A company that sticks with you,* I don't care about the company. Focus on what people get, on their benefits.

My rule of thumb in writing any copy is, *Get out of your ego, and get into the customer's ego.* The second one is about the company's ego. I don't care about the company, although the company does. They wrote the ad, and they were probably proud of themselves. The first option focuses on the person and the product.

Next:

1. *Double your income in three years.*
2. *How to sell your way into the big money.*

Here again, the first is more hypnotic. It's very specific. How-tos are very powerful, but when you get down to the specifics and you can say, *Double your income in three years,* that's it. There is the statement. It's very hypnotic, isn't it?

"They Laughed When I . . ."

One of the most famous ads in history was written in 1925 by John Caples: "*They laughed when I sat down at the piano—but when I started to play!*"

As I've said, we're called copywriters because we copy. We learn from other people. We have our own files of other people's work that we admire, and we adapt it to our needs when the moment is right.

This famous headline has been adapted quite a bit. Some examples:

"*They laughed when I said they could have perfect pitch until I showed them the secret.*" This ad is for a system that teaches you how to recognize musical notes by ear. They adapted John Caples' headline. You can too.

"*They laughed when I used my headphones to meditate, but when they saw the results, they all begged to try it.*"

"*They all laughed when I said I was going to start my own business.*"

Do you see how you can use this concept?

Do you think this is a good ad? "*Use the time-tested secrets of tycoons, titans, and billionaires to explode your business profits in 90 days.*" Do you think that's a hypnotic ad? You'd better. It's for my program. It's my ad.

Some people ask, "Is it too long?" As long as people are reading and responding to it, it's not too long.

This is another topic that comes up. People often say that copy is too long. Sometimes you'll get sales letters that are thirty-two pages long. Is that too long? Not if it sells. After all, don't people read books? Don't they read magazine articles? Don't they read long things as long as they're interesting? If they didn't read your copy, it wasn't interesting to them. Length doesn't really matter. I work very hard to make my writing as concise as possible. But my rule of thumb is, in general, the higher the amount of money I'm asking for, the longer the copy needs to be.

If I asked you to have lunch with me, you'd probably say yes. If I said, "Come and have lunch with me, and bring $10 with you," you'd probably still say yes. But if I said, "Come and have lunch with me. Bring $10,000. I want to tell you about something I've got to sell you," you'd want to know why. Long sales copy comes into play when I've got to explain what I'm offering.

Next: *"At last! Discover the success secrets of the forgotten genius who made men presidents, tycoons, and heads of empires."*

It's my ad, and I think it's pretty good. I also came up with a guarantee: *"Your guarantee: Use these seven principles for six months. If you're out of work, you'll get a job. If you're employed, you'll get a raise. If you're in business, you'll see a whopping 25 percent jump in revenues—or return this book and you'll receive a full-cash refund."*

The book has gone through numerous editions. Nobody has ever turned in the book and asked for a refund.

I think more of us have to be bold in our guarantees. We have to put the risk on ourselves and take it off customers, because most people are very lazy. Even if they don't like your product, they probably won't return it. (Not that you want to sell shoddy products; I'm not suggesting that at all.)

My software is called the Hypnotic Writing Wizard. It was created by Calvin Chapman. It's based on my first two best-selling e-books, *Hypnotic Writing* and *Advanced Hypnotic Writing*. It's got templates that'll help you write sales letters, ads, news releases, web copy, talks for books, and talks for speaking, even entire books.

Here are some sample headlines:

"*What is now the easiest way in the world to write a sales letter, ad, flyer, brochure, news release, article, speech, web copy, or even an entire book, guaranteed, fast, and for free?*"

"*Announcing Dr. Joe Vitale's Hypnotic Writing Wizard.*"

"*Who is the Hypnotic Writing Wizard? You are when you use this incredible new software.*"

I've discussed these headlines with audiences. They thought the first one was wordy, although I liked it. This goes to show that the public rules here. When you fall in love with your ads, you're making a mistake. You need to let the public vote on them. It does not matter if Joe likes the first one. If it doesn't get the response, it's history.

"*Announcing Dr. Joe Vitale's Hypnotic Writing Wizard*": this didn't get much response.

How about "*Who is the Hypnotic Writing Wizard?*" It's good, but the second part gives the answer away. If you bury it and send the reader to your website to find out, it's likely to be a winner.

10
Hypnotic Advertising

*I*f new hair doesn't grow after using my method—I don't want a penny." This is the headline for an ad from 1923. Notice how the headline targets exactly who the market is: men who are bald. When you create sales materials, you want to target that way too.

Another feature: *"I don't want a penny."* There's a guarantee. Guarantees are big. Guarantee everything you do. I think you're required by law anyway to do it for thirty days, but guarantee everything you do. It's going to make a big difference in your results.

Another ad headline: *Is your head only a hair farm?* Is that a good one or a bad one?

It's bad. It doesn't tell you what it's about. It's very misleading. You may well think the product has to do with hair or hair restoration. It's actually selling a book, but you can't tell that. This headline tries to be cute. Cute and clever does not sell, or very rarely sells. Stay away from cute and clever. Go for direct benefits.

When people are looking at your sales materials, they give them a split second. They don't spend any time on the materials that you're paying a lot of money for them to look at. If you don't communicate what you're offering, you lose.

What about this? "*When doctors feel rotten, this is what they do!*" Is this good or bad?

It's actually excellent. This is a famous ad. Why does it use the words "feel rotten"? How come they just didn't say, "When doctors feel bad," "When doctors are sick," or "When doctors are ill"?

They want to go for the emotions. "Feel rotten" elicits an emotional response in people. People don't buy unless you've involved them emotionally. Then they justify what they're buying with logic. That's why there needs to be different kinds of material, like testimonials and guarantees, to make it easy for them to buy. But you have to tap into their emotions before they'll pay attention, before they'll actually want it. "Feel rotten" is very emotional. They're excellent words.

This is a famous ad from the 1950s.

I don't know who you are.

I don't know your company.

I don't know your company's product.

I don't know what your company stands for.

I don't know your company's customers.

I don't know your company's record.

I don't know your company's reputation.

Now, what is it that you wanted to sell me?

This is why you have to have marketing documents out there: to sell you before you get to the door or before you call the customer. They inform people about who you are and what you do. You need business cards, brochures, ads, flyers, postcards, and sales materials, and this proves it. Does the guy who's speaking in this ad sound like a guy you want to talk to? Not today. He needs to be sold on who you are and what you're doing.

If you want your ad to stand out, you have to do something that's going to make it stand out. Say you are running a classified or small display ad in the back of a magazine. You know the easiest way to write one of these? Just hammer on the benefit or the problem. If anybody has a headache, the only ad that would jump out here would probably be the one that said, "Headache Relief." That's what they're interested in. Don't go for anything cute. You want to make it as direct, as benefit-oriented, as simple, as rifle-shot as it can be.

"Make words work for you." This was the beginning of a series that led to a famous ad in the 1920s. They

started with this one. These were professional copywriters, who don't write these things in one sitting and quit. They spend a lot of time looking for the unique angle, the unique emotional benefit, and for the headline that's going to bring it.

The copywriters didn't settle for this headline. They noted how many responses they got. Then they created another ad for the same thing.

The next ad said, *"New way to find and correct your mistakes in English—only 15 minutes a day."* Again, they're testing: which one is the better of the two?

Another attempt: *"Make your language win for you."* These people were shelling out real money to do this. In the 1920s, it cost a phenomenal amount of money to advertise. But they knew it was important enough to keep testing.

We need to do the same thing. When you come up with a flyer, a headline, an ad, a headline, or a brochure, be willing to change it, improve it, test it. It was good enough for those ad men. It could be good enough for us.

The copywriters still were not done. They came up with *"What does your English tell about you?"* Questions are good for headlines. I love questions if they get you involved. With the question in this headline, you have to read a little further to understand what it's talking about. It's pulling people into the copy.

The copywriters did not stop there. *"Make your English win for you."* This is starting to target people.

Another attempt for the same product: *"His simple invention has shown thousands how to break bad habits in English."* In the course of this series, the writers were also constantly changing ad size, typeface, subheads, pictures—still testing.

The copywriters ended up with this: *"Do you make these mistakes in English?"* This is one of the most famous advertisements in history. Once the writers got here, they stayed there for forty years. They did not change it again. But they had tested all of those earlier versions first.

These are the versions I know about. The writers may have tested more, but once they decided that this was the winner, they stuck with it and didn't change. Stay with the winning racehorse. They did for forty years.

Use simple and direct language. The average reading level of the American public is around that of the seventh or eighth grade. So you don't want to make your writing complicated. Most writers use a thesaurus to find a bigger word for what they're trying to express. Do the opposite. Find a smaller word. Something with only one syllable would be best.

Generally speaking, the more you tell, the more you sell. The tests say that longer copy will pull better results for you. Now that doesn't mean mindlessly filling up the page with words, because the real work is making this copy irresistible reading.

People are reading books, magazines, and long articles. As long as you are interesting the people this is targeted for, they will read every word. Advertising legend David Ogilvy said that it's when you step into boredom that they stop reading. That's why copywriters get paid so much. They're supposed to know how to write irresistibly, grab attention with the headline, and keep the audience reading all the way through. There was a full page in *The New York Times* that had 7,000 words in small type. Yet it pulled so well that it only ran one time, and 100,000 people responded to it.

You might want to consider creating an ad or a brochure in an editorial style—an advertorial. The magazine usually puts the word "advertisement" at the top, but people still see it and read it as a story. Although we live in the age of skepticism, people tend to trust what they read in newspapers and magazines, so an advertorial has legitimacy. If you make your copy look like what they're reading in a newspaper or magazine, even with the word "advertisement" at the top, they will trust it more.

At the end, you have a description of the author, a bio box, or a resource box, as it's often called. It gives your name, address, and what you've written. It's like having a coupon.

Sometimes I'll create an ad and the client will say, "I want more white space in the ad." Look at the newspapers. How much white space do they leave? They know if they come up with some news, a headline, an illustration, you'll read it. Why, then, will an advertiser who has to pay big bucks for the same space not put anything in it?

"Let's make it white." No. In fact, some tests have shown that a cluttered, busy-looking, word-filled ad outpulls one that has fewer words in it and looks more orderly. For one thing, the first one is going to get more attention. Again, you don't want to just throw things in there. You don't want to write copy that's weak or boring. It all has to work. But in general, the more you tell, the more you sell.

Here are some more sample ads. *"How to ruin your marriage in the quickest possible way."* Is this a good ad?

No. This ad is not good. It bombed. From an attention-getting standpoint, the headline probably does stop people in their tracks and maybe chuckle a little bit. But who wants to buy a way to ruin your marriage? Somebody cracked, "You don't even need a book for that."

How-to headlines typically work. David Ogilvy is a master. Here are some of the how-to ads that he wrote: *"How to create corporate advertising that gets results." "How to launch new products." "How to make your self-promotions more profitable." "How much should you spend on advertising?" "How to advertise Travel." "How to create food adver-*

tising that sells." All of these were advertisements for his service.

Give people what they want. They will read it. They will read all of those words. They will be impressed. They will learn something. And if you've truly sold them, when they get down at the bottom and see the coupon or the phone number, they will contact you.

This is the headline of a flyer for a book: *"As long as life."* Is that good or bad? I would say it's bad. "As long as life"—what does that mean? What does that tell you? Nothing.

Here's a fun one.

1. *Why clown around in black and white when you can do it in color just as easily?*

2. *These are just a few of 16,777,216 colors your PCAT can process using our color frame grabber.*

They're both for the same thing. They were tested. Which did better, 1 or 2?

The second is actually the big winner. Let's look at this closely. If you look at the headline for 1, what are they talking about? We don't know. This option doesn't clearly and directly communicate what you're selling.

The second one does. A number gives a lot of credibility. And a big odd number like that creates believability. The first one doesn't have anything like that. The second one also says "your." Remember that *you* and *your* are power words. The first one is cuter, but it bombed.

What do you think of this one? "*He who talks first wins.*" It's intriguing, it's curious, it's different. But from taking one glance, can you tell what it's about? Can you tell what the benefit is? It's for a negotiating course, but would you know that? A subhead and testimonials might help.

When I'm done writing copy, I go through a number of steps to make sure that I've written it well. Does the opening begin with a bang? Is this the best that you can do? It's too easy to say yes. Remember that whole series of ads for improved language power? They paid to test every one of them. There was a half dozen of them before they got to the winner. Be willing to go back to make your work the best it can be.

Be willing to get feedback from your peers. Even more importantly, ask a few of your customers to look at your copy. If a targeted prospect says, "I want this," you know you've got a winner.

Make sure you don't have a weak headline or, worse, no headline. Having no headline is the worst sin of all. You use the headline to attract the right audience with a clear benefit to them. By now, you should be aware that that's what we're going for, how to do it, and what to look for.

Reveal as many benefits as you can using active writing in an exciting and personal style. Again, you want to write copy that conveys in a simple way what you're talking about. Also, rewrite, rewrite, rewrite. Test, test, test.

Finally, in order to generate more sales, think of what your customer gets, not what you want to sell. That is the single most important distinction. Remember my little hypnotic phrase: *get out of your ego, and get into your customer's ego.*

I think I'm done. Thank you very much. Go out and make millions from what you've just learned.

About the Author

D r. Joe Vitale is a globally famous author, marketing guru, movie, TV, and radio personality, musician, and one of the top 50 inspirational speakers in the world.

His many bestselling books include *The Attractor Factor*, *Attract Money Now*, *Zero Limits*, *The Miracle: Six Steps to Enlightenment*, and *Anything Is Possible*.

He's also recorded numerous bestselling audio programs, from The Missing Secret and The Zero Point to The Power of Outrageousness Marketing and The Awakening Course.

A popular, leading expert on the law of attraction in many hit movies, including The Secret, Dr. Vitale discovered the "missing secret" not revealed in the movie. He's been on Larry King Live, Donny Deutsch's "The Big Idea," CNN, CNBC, CBS, ABC, Fox News: Fox & Friends and

Extra TV. He's also been featured in *The New York Times* and *Newsweek*.

One of his most recent accomplishments includes being the world's first self-help singer-songwriter as seen in 2012's *Rolling Stone Magazine*. To date, he has released seventeen albums! Several of his songs were recognized and nominated for the Posi Award, regarded as "The Grammys of Positive Music."

Well-known not only as a thinker, but as a healer, clearing people's subconscious minds of limiting beliefs, Dr. Joe Vitale is also an authentic practitioner of modern Ho'oponopono, certified Reiki healer, certified Chi Kung practitioner, certified Clinical Hypnotherapist, certified NLP practitioner, Ordained Minister, and Doctor of Metaphysical Science.

He is a seeker and a learner; once homeless, he has spent the last four decades learning how to master the powers that channel the pure creative energy of life without resistance, and created the Miracles Coaching® and Zero Limits Mastery® programs to help people achieve their life's purpose. He lives outside Austin, Texas, with his love, Lisa Winston.

His main site is www.MrFire.com.

He is the host of the popular online weekly TV show, "Zero Limits Living." See www.ZeroLimitsLivingTV.com.

CPSIA information can be obtained
at www.ICGtesting.com
Printed in the USA
JSHW041350130222
22871JS00003B/3

9 781722 505745